Designin With—in Public Organizations

Building Bridges Between
Public Sector Innovators
and Designers

D1591587

André
Schaminée

Forword by
Kees Dorst

From Words to Deeds

People tend to believe that a good idea will automatically lead to the desired change. But that's not true.

In today's society, public organizations, companies and citizens have a new relationship with each other. We live together and operate in continuously changing networks. This creates some amazing opportunities, but also some unique new headaches. What does a healthy network society look like? How do we structure it? How do we collaborate in a network? The only thing we know for sure is that the trusted ways of tackling issues no longer work. In our rapidly changing world, best practices that were successful in the past no longer offer any guarantees.

The development of a network society presents major challenges for everyone, but in particular for organizations in the public sector. These organizations suddenly find themselves unintentionally on the front line of this transformation, and they're not designed to deal with it. Core values like equality before the law, precision and efficiency have helped guide a reliable public sector for a long time. Now these values could be impeding the public sector's transformation and journey towards a new era.

Time will not solve this problem as a matter of course. Instead, this requires originality and a fresh perspective. In their search for such a new dynamic, more and more public organizations are turning to artists and designers. This is perfectly understandable: after all, the question of how we want to live together in a network society is a design question.

As a result, a wealth of courses and seminars on design thinking has emerged that teach participants to think outside the box. Designers have a useful toolbox of methods and techniques to create new insights and generate ideas. But if you then decide in an outside-the-box way to rid yourself of old patterns of thinking and come up with new ideas, you come face to face with the hard everyday reality of a second, much more difficult box, i.e. the organization that is part of the problem and that cannot or will not change.

As innovative thinkers, designers tend to believe that a good idea will automatically lead to the desired change. But that's not true. Confronted with the powers that want to keep everything as it is, designing unfortunately doesn't offer the answer—designing stops at the idea. Developing new ideas using design thinking is a good start, but it's no more than a first step on the long journey from being right to being proven right and getting your way. In our enthusiasm, we underestimate how long and arduous that journey can be.

In this book, André Schaminée outlines how we can take things further and move from words to deeds. We can benefit from his unique perspective as a consultant working in the twilight zone between the world of designing and the world of public organizations. André is the ideal person for this: he has one foot in the design world and the other in the world of organizational consultancy, and is one of the very few people who know how to bridge the gap between these two worlds.

This book explains the nature of that gap and how wide it is, something that is often underestimated. Using real examples, the book illustrates how a keen insight, strategic approach and sometimes a healthy dose of learning on the job can help advance ideas. This requires knowledge, expertise, a pragmatic take on the world, smart leadership and sometimes a lot of patience. By following the guidance in this book, a good idea really can lead to change.

KEES DORST
Professor of Design Innovation
University of Technology Sydney

Table of Content

Introduction

There aren't enough instruments and tools where organizations and design intersect. Moreover, there isn't even a profession for this field of work yet.

A NEW APPROACH
TO PUBLIC ISSUES

More and more of the issues the public sector[1] is facing can barely be resolved by the sector itself—if at all—with generic policy measures also proving insufficient. For instance, how do you ensure that young people can develop their talents? That we're prepared for climate change? That the level of vaccination against diseases remains high enough? These are (social) issues that no one entirely understands and that cannot be effectively addressed by any one person[2].

These types of issues are 'networked', i.e. they're linked to a whole range of other issues. As such, solutions don't work if they're generic; rather, they only work if they're specific to situations. These issues are dynamic, which means they change while you're working on them. Solutions, as a result, are never achieved. Moreover, the issues are open, in that different parties can access them. That means that solutions can only be realized when everyone affected by the issue is given the opportunity to become part of the solution— everyone on their own terms[3].

Public sector staff also realize that in many places rules have become more important than people, while it's those very rules that should actually be helping people progress. There's a widespread desire to place end-users[4] centre stage again, i.e. have more of a life-world and less of a systems world.

This explains the rationale of the innovators in the public sector to find new approaches to deal with wicked problems. Design thinking is one example of this. It places people (and not systems) centre stage. It helps to embrace complexity instead of knocking it down. Design thinking literally allows us to look at issues differently. What's more, this approach turns innovative ideas into small, effective iterative steps, thereby increasing the likelihood of change.

WORKING ON A NEW DISCOURSE

Public organizations are increasingly curious about what design thinking can mean for resolving social issues. More and more are experimenting with this approach, which has already led to countless significant developments in terms of safety, food, health and infrastructure.

At the same time, there are increasing insights into the fact that design thinking is noticeably different to the processes that public sector staff are used to using to resolve issues. These differences still stand in the way of design thinking being successfully employed. Thankfully, these differences can be bridged. This does, however, require attention, care and a new, unifying discourse. Or as Prof. Kees Dorst[5] once stated: "There's a lack of instruments and tools where organizations and design intersect. Moreover, there's not even a profession for that area."

That discourse is being worked on in several areas. For instance, there are government authorities that organize design training sessions and there are university management and business courses that work together with design courses. Also, design and art courses are increasingly encouraging their students to do projects in the public sector. These sorts of initiatives are powerful and broaden the horizon of everyone involved. They also teach us that there's still a lot to learn and discover.

Building and maintaining the right context for a design-thinking process in public organizations is a new, barely explored field. Although a significant number of people are already doing meaningful, unifying work in this area in an intuitive manner, it will help a lot to make those ways of working explicit. This will make design thinking in the public sector more powerful and successful.

In the past ten years, I've looked at the collaborations between designers and public organizations through the prism of organizational science. I've made a career out of building and maintaining the right context for a design process within public organizations. This book shares the insights I've gained, which I hope contribute to building a foundation for a unifying discourse between designers and public organizations, and which I hope encourages readers to seek out and share their own experiences.

WHO'S THIS BOOK FOR?

This book is intended as an educational reference book for designers who want their work to have an impact on social issues and thereby enter into a relationship with public organizations. Public sector staff experimenting with design, or who intend to do so, may also find the book beneficial. It will give them a better understanding of how they can make design thinking a success in their day-to-day work.

The third target group is people working in the field between design thinking and public organizations, i.e. people building the context in which design thinking is becoming a success. There are more than enough issues in the public sector for which a design approach is proving promising. Also, there are many designers who aspire to solve these issues. For the time being, however, what's missing is people to help build that context and bridge the gap between design thinking and organizational processes: from formulating a re-search question to conducting the research itself, designing a concept, creating the prototype and implementing it. Those 'context builders' are that 'missing profession': a profession with a future.

READING GUIDE

Design thinking is a very broad concept. As such, this book first explains what I'm talking about when I refer to design thinking. Chapter 1 then outlines various types of issues and explains where a collaboration between designers and public organizations offers the most promise.

Chapters 2 through 5 explain how design thinking differs from traditional approaches in the public sector to issues, describing what added value it brings, but also what tensions it introduces. In this case, my arguments are based on organizational science models and principles, illustrated with a number of practical experiences. Chapter 2 reflects on change, while chapter 3 talks about collaborations. Chapter 4 examines the crucial role in a design project played by the 'boundary spanners' at organizations and chapter 5 looks at power and the sources of power.

Finally, chapter 6 explores the working relationship between designers and public organizations at four stages in the design process, namely formulating the research question, empathic research, reframing and prototyping. Which flanking interventions are required in the process to increase the likelihood of the final proposals being successfully implemented?

This book builds on various methods and techniques used in the design world, as well as some knowledge and concepts from management and organizational science. Where necessary, it provides further reading suggestions.

Chapter 1

Public Organizations and Wicked Problems

Design thinking gives public organizations the tools for approaching problems in a new way. But for design thinking to be applied successfully, it must first be clear to stakeholders what design thinking actually entails and for which issues this approach is suitable. This chapter defines a few terms and outlines for which issues this way of working can be of added value.

The thing with wicked problems is that what's allowed doesn't work, and what works isn't allowed.

Hans Vermaak

CROSSING THE BOUNDARY
BETWEEN DESIGN AND
ORGANIZATIONAL CONSULTING

The business cards of people I've worked with over the past few years say things like 'design thinker', 'social designer' and 'service designer'. My network includes alumni from art and design courses, as well as alumni from technical universities. What connects them all is their desire as designers to find solutions to social issues. They share the conviction that aesthetics and technology serve a greater social purpose. In this case, they're in tune with designer Victor Papanek, who said "only a small part of our responsibility lies in the area of aesthetics."[6]

The designers I work with realize they cannot retreat to the safety of their own studio or academy when dealing with social issues, but instead have to implement co-creative processes with all stakeholders. That could be end-users like patients, tenants or students, depending on the issue at hand. But more often than not, the stakeholders also include organizations, and as part of the design process, they, too, must be involved in the problem and the solution. As such, my team's motto is: everyone who's part of the problem should be able to be part of the change.

In my world, i.e. the world of organizational consulting, designers are a pretty new and unknown phenomena. How will a designer work within traditional areas of consultancy like change management, collaboration and strategic management? And yet, it's not all that strange an idea to link design and designers with this practice. Designers introduce a new repertoire that everyday practice yearns for, and in turn organizational science gives designers tools to realize their process and implement the effects thereof. In other words: to have it lead to an impactful change.

SOCIAL DESIGN, DESIGN THINKING…
WHAT'S IN A NAME?

In the 2014 study *SOCIALDESIGNFORWICKEDPROBLEMS*[7], Tabo Goudswaard, Klaas Kuitenbrouwer and I used the term 'social design'. This term is at the heart of what this book talks about. It's about design processes and solutions that have been created to have a positive influence on society's wellbeing. That said, 'social design' is also a term with many limitations. Can 'service design' also be 'social design'? And isn't every good design actually in principle 'social design'?

Another term that's used a lot (and equally maligned) is 'design thinking'. This term is used everywhere and refers to methods and techniques that designers use to achieve innovative solutions. The resistance to this term is due to the emphasis on 'thinking', among other things. After all, design is as much about the 'doing'. What's more, 'design thinking' has also become associated with such superficial practices that real designers no longer recognize themselves in the term.

In this book, I don't address this discussion and instead use the most popular term: 'design thinking'. I may sometimes only use the word 'design', with which I mean the same thing. I also talk variously about the design process and the design-thinking process. I often refer to the professionals in this field as designers. I think it's more important to understand the types of issues you can deal with using design thinking and how you can achieve effective solutions than having a discussion about word choice. In which case, let me begin with the first question.

FOUR ORDERS
OF DESIGN

Design has developed a lot over the years and has almost organically turned into a practice that is very appropriate for

Fig. 1:   Four orders of design.

FOUR ORDERS
OF DESIGN

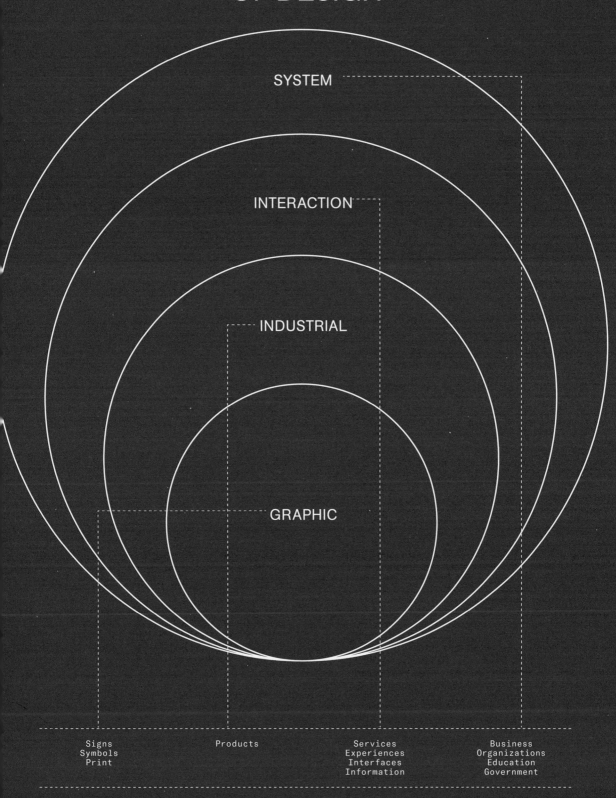

SYSTEM

INTERACTION

INDUSTRIAL

GRAPHIC

Signs
Symbols
Print

Products

Services
Experiences
Interfaces
Information

Business
Organizations
Education
Government

Everyone
who's part
of the problem
should be
able to be part
of the solution.

the issues facing our society today. Richard Buchanan, for instance, illustrates this nicely with his definition of the four orders of design[8] (see figure 1).

In his model, the first order of design comprises communication with symbols and illustrations. In the past, there was a horseshoe and a plough, for instance; there was little difference between the job and the design.

The second order arises when products are no longer created in the places they are used, but in factories instead. To sell these, people have to think about aesthetics, functionality and meaning, but also about marketing and communication. The manufacturer is no longer the designer and the communicator. Design agencies are established outside the factories.

In the middle of the 20th century, the idea arose that design could also be applied to activities and processes. This is what Buchanan calls the third order of design, and in essence this is about interaction and communication. This type of design is generally outsourced by organizations to external parties.

And finally, the fourth order. This is the design of systems and environments in which the other orders of design can exist. To design such systems and environments requires that you understand the big systems, in ideological, practical and pragmatic terms. Capitalism is not constructed in the same way as socialism. The Rhine capitalism model is different to the Anglo-Saxon one. And even within these large systems there's a huge range of phenomena. These are often very much related to culture, time, place and individuals. Part of the fourth order of design is to understand how these systems work and on what core values, convictions and authorities they are founded. Issues in this case include: How can you get patients to work on their own health themselves? How should we deal with climate change? As such, what shape the solutions will take at the start is still unclear.

The design of relationships also falls under the fourth order of design. For instance, the relationships between healthcare

FOUR TYPES
OF ISSUES

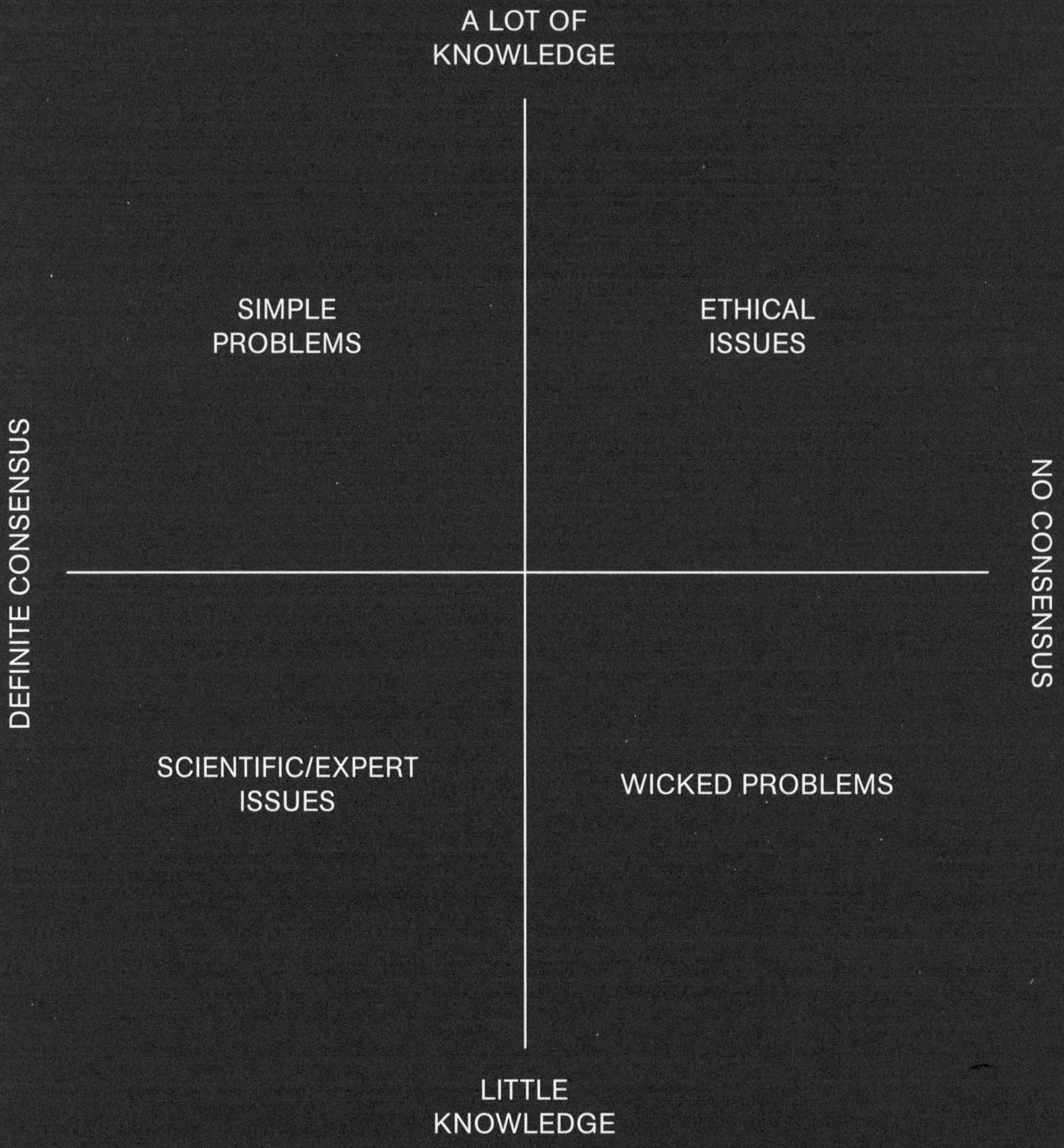

A LOT OF
KNOWLEDGE

SIMPLE
PROBLEMS

ETHICAL
ISSUES

DEFINITE CONSENSUS

NO CONSENSUS

SCIENTIFIC/EXPERT
ISSUES

WICKED PROBLEMS

LITTLE
KNOWLEDGE

institutions and patients, between schools and students, between building projects and the living environment or—to be more generic—the relationship between a government and citizens. Services can be viewed as the materialization of this relationship. As such, service design projects are often fourth order issues.

The organizations, i.e. systems, are part of the problem. Fourth order issues cannot, therefore, be isolated from the environments in which they exist and as such cannot be outsourced by organizations. The designer has to work with and within the organizations in question. As such, a designer working on a system change has to know about the systems. And vice versa: the client has to know about the design process to be able to successfully implement it in the organization. A design process must be introduced into the primary processes to be able to facilitate change.

A DESIGN APPROACH ISN'T SUITABLE FOR EVERY ISSUE

This book places third and fourth order issues centre stage. Although a man with a hammer often sees the world as a nail, not all third and fourth order issues are automatically also design issues. Indeed, in many cases an approach other than a design approach is far more effective.

The 2008 model by Professor Arno Korsten[9] illustrates this very well. He plots issues on two axes: the first axis represents the degree of consensus, while the second axis represents the amount of available knowledge. The two axes create four quadrants (see figure 2).

The first quadrant contains simple problems. There's a lot of knowledge and a lot of consensus on solving problems like these, e.g. the fight against measles. We know a lot about this disease and there's a vaccine that can be used, with no significant side effects. The risk of a measles epidemic is, in principle, sufficiently under control thanks to a project-based approach, i.e. ensure the vaccines are available so that children can be vaccinated in time and the level of vaccination is high enough to protect the entire population. This requires activities and processes, but the expertise of designers adds very little.

A simple problem doesn't always behave that way however. Vaccinating is a contentious issue among orthodox religions, although the danger of the disease and the effect of the vaccine are not necessarily underestimated. As such, a simple problem becomes an ethical issue and ends up in the second quadrant, where there's a lot of knowledge, but no consensus. This means a new discourse on the facts needs to be developed, with people's values and convictions being used as the foundation for establishing accepted knowledge. Here, too, a design approach is not the most logical. The problem would benefit more from a social debate than a (re)design.

The respiratory syncytial virus (RSV) virus is an example that amply illustrates the third quadrant. We know there are 33 million children around the world under the age of five with a respiratory infection caused by the RSV virus and that 120,000 of these children die every year[10]. What we don't know, however, is how the disease can be treated or prevented. The biggest problem with this issue concerns the gathering of (scientific) knowledge. Once again, the role that designers can play in this is limited.

The fourth quadrant includes the issue of people who cast doubt on the effect and the desirability of the measles vaccine. These people may also doubt the severity of the disease. In particular, there's a growing resistance in society to the preventive vaccination of children, not least among the well-educated. What complicates this is that this resistance is anything but simple. Some opponents have no faith in the independence or the quality of science, while others distrust the government. And then there are those people who think the risk the disease poses is exaggerated. Despite the fact that people cannot disprove the knowledge of scientists, they cast doubt on it. As a result, there's no accepted knowledge or consensus that can be used to advance the situation. And it's precisely with these sorts of issues that designers can bring added value.

FOCUS ON WICKED PROBLEMS

Issues that fall into Korsten's fourth quadrant are ones that I call 'wicked problems'. These are (social) issues that no one entirely understands and that cannot be effectively addressed by any one person. Wicked problems have at least four traits[11] in common. They are:

↳ Dynamic: they change as you work on them.
↳ Open: they're accessible to many.
↳ Networked: they can rarely be resolved by a single organization or within an individual pillar.
↳ Complex: simple solutions are not effective or permitted.

The last example in the previous section is an apt illustration of this. Resistance to the measles vaccination is a cause for concern among paediatricians. They have to deal with parents who are using counterarguments they've found on Google. These arguments can vary from "internet forums tell me that that the likelihood of autism is far greater than you're saying" to "everyone knows that big pharma pays for scientific research." Refuting these arguments has little effect because this doesn't deal with the underlying mistrust.

The most important guarantee to preventing an epidemic is to ensure a high vaccination level among the population. But who's responsible for that? An individual paediatrician can't take on that responsibility. So who can?

A simple solution such as making vaccination mandatory is not widely supported in the Netherlands, unlike in some of neighbouring countries. Any similar suggestions lead to an ethical discussion in which—up to now—human autonomy

In a traditionally managed organization, the introduction of design thinking will lead to conflicts.

carries the most weight. In short, more knowledge won't help resolve this wicked problem. Further debates won't help either. Something different is required in this case. Design thinking can offer a deep insight into what motivates the stakeholders and holds them back, and the ability to co-create a new narrative based on this insight.

THE QUICK APPROACH:
JUMPING TO SOLUTIONS

Applying design thinking to wicked problems may seem very promising, but that doesn't mean it's easy to set up a well-thought-out design-thinking process at public organizations. There are two reasons for this. In general, public organizations are still not very enthusiastic about dealing with wicked problems. After all, wicked problems are (social) issues that no one entirely understands and that cannot be effectively addressed by any one person. As such, they're not easy to manage in the traditional sense of the word and in a public organization that's managed in a traditional manner it's risky to tie yourself to one of these issues. Before you know it, you're responsible for an issue that you actually can't take responsibility for[12].

More importantly, people in public organizations are often not yet familiar with a design-thinking process. The methods, the tools and the mentality can all differ from what people are used to. As such, setting to work with design thinking can make it even more difficult for stakeholders to manage the process. If you haven't totally figured out both the issue and the approach you want to use to solve the issue, it's very difficult to keep control.

As a result, public sector staff working in a coalition with designers may quickly try to get a handle on the process by aiming for a clear end point. At least then people will know what their goal is. In this case, there's little scope for a thorough design process and the focus ends up being on quickly finding clear and safe answers, i.e. people jumping to solutions. There's no issue with speed—design thinking is not a long-term process per-se—but it can be an issue if there's too much emphasis on finding a solution instead of focussing on properly understanding the problem.

One risk of an approach that's too focused on finding a solution is that the existing way of looking at the issue is not discussed, while it's exactly that way of looking that may be keeping the issue alive. Jumping to solutions is contrary to Einstein's law: everything should be made as simple as possible, but not simpler. In their work with public organizations, designers often feel under pressure to deliver answers quickly.

But what also happens is that they, too, have too superficial a design approach on offer. Professor Thomas Fisher of the University of Minnesota[13] puts it like this: "We see this all the time: workshops filled with post-it notes and led by a 'design' person who takes the audience through abstract activities that have little to do with the actual challenges facing the participants or their organization. While getting people outside of their comfort zone can create an environment that fosters creativity, design thinking must respond to the political, financial and cultural realities of the organizations it engages. Otherwise, it can become empty busywork that frustrates more than it empowers."

THE THOROUGH APPROACH:
FRAME INNOVATION

There are several design approaches that can be used to deal with wicked problems. Many encompass four basic phases that are generally referred to as 'understanding', 'empathizing', 'ideation' and 'prototyping'. The understanding phase seeks to understand how an issue manifests itself and who it involves. The empathizing phase examines what motivates those people involved. In the ideation phase, new strategies and ideas are developed, and through prototyping these are turned into efficient proposals that can ultimately be tested and applied.

This classification offers scope for both superficial and thorough approaches, with practice showing that the risk of jumping to solutions, as described in the above section, is the greatest in the ideation phase.

A thorough design-thinking approach is frame innovation, as developed by Professor Kees Dorst[14].

FRAME INNOVATION

The basic idea behind frame innovation is that a shared outlook on an issue, i.e. a frame, connects people and organizations to find measures and solutions in a process of co-creation. Reframing an issue is something that wicked problems nearly always need because the predominant way of looking at the issue has generally contributed to it becoming a wicked problem in the first place.

There are nine steps to frame innovation, see figure 3. The first five, i.e. archaeology, paradox, context, field and themes, lead to the reframing. The sixth step is the reframing itself; after that come three more steps, i.e. futures, transformation and integration, that examine the potential of the new frame.

The archaeology step examines how the problem is perceived, its history (i.e. how the problem arose) and what

attempts have already been made to solve the problem.

The formulation of the central paradox should ensure a clear understanding of what makes the problem a wicked problem. Why can't it simply be solved?

The next two steps concern empathic research, i.e. understanding at a deep level what motivates the stakeholders. The context step focuses on the immediate stakeholders and the parties clearly required for a solution. The field step extends that research to potential important parties, i.e., parties who could be connected to the problem.

Empathic research provides the building blocks for the next step: the formulation of universal (and thereby unifying), deeper underlying and intrinsic themes that the stakeholders find important. It should be noted that the way in which the themes manifest can vary enormously between stakeholders.

The deeper underlying themes can then be used as input for creating a new perspective, i.e. the so-called frames. This is one of the most creative moments in the entire process. The deeper underlying themes are not new to the world; there are other situations where these play a role and where people have learned to handle them successfully. These situations are taken as a new way of looking at things.

The future step examines the promise and importance of new solutions arising from the new frame. The transformation step looks at what the solutions mean for the stakeholders' daily practices and what's needed to really get a solution implemented.

Finally, the integration step collates the lessons learned from the successful application of the new frame. What additional opportunities does it present stakeholders with?

For me, the thoroughness of frame innovation is due to a number of factors. The wickedness of the problem is fully examined during the archaeology step. This prevents answers that had previously been thought of from being thought of later in the process and from solutions being devised that had already clearly been shown to be unfeasible or unusable. The step identifying the central paradox helps to clearly establish that you're dealing with the essence of the issue. The step investigating the deeper underlying themes allows for 'not knowing', with everything hanging in the air, so to speak. This step includes an important part of the thoroughness that other approaches sometimes lose during the ideation stage. And last, but certainly not least: the (re)framing step is the essence of this approach and places the development of a new way of looking at the issue centre stage. This step is crucial for wicked problems because there are generally no more effective solutions available in the predominant way of looking at things.

Fig. 3: The nine steps of frame innovation.

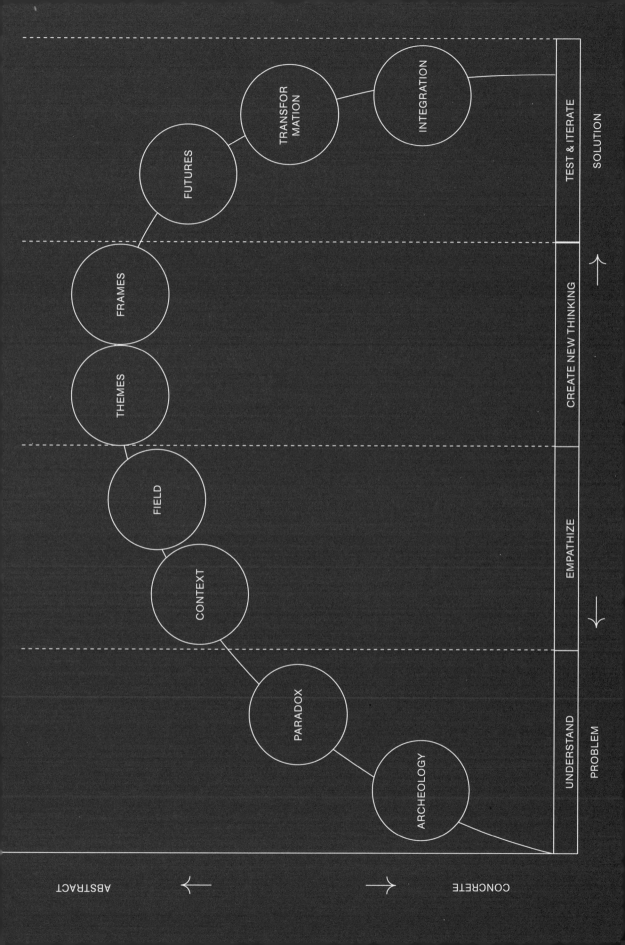

In my work, I prefer to use the frame innovation approach. The advantage of this approach is that it's thorough and the steps to be taken are easy for non-designers to understand — provided they're well supervised of course.

FOCUS ON THE PUBLIC SECTOR

There's a real need at many organizations to look for new approaches to deal with wicked problems. A thorough design-thinking process is one such very promising approach, but, as mentioned earlier, it's no easy task to really bring this approach to life when working with organizations that are managed in a traditional fashion. This applies to all organizations: public, semi-public and private. That said, there are a number of key differences between public and private organizations when it comes to creating the right context for a successful process.

To start with, the public sector has a responsibility to citizens. That creates a different, more complex dynamic compared to having to be accountable to shareholders. What's more, innovation is part of the DNA of companies. If it isn't, they simply don't survive. That's different for the public sector. Without wanting to underestimate the role the public sector plays in innovation, government authorities have an almost natural resistance to change and innovation. This resistance plays a role — which I'll come back to later — but also means there's a lot more attention and energy needed to break down barriers between the primary (policy) processes and an innovative design process. As such, this book doesn't discuss organizations in general, but focuses on public organizations.

Design thinking is both an inviting perspective for public organizations as well as an intervention in the way they work on change, the way in which they collaborate and the resources they commit to that. Design thinking also breaks through the barrier between inside and outside, between the lifeworld and the systems world. Chapters 2 through 5 will cover this in detail.

Key Ideas in This Chapter

↪ Public organizations are increasingly facing wicked problems; these are (social) issues that no one entirely understands and that cannot be effectively addressed by any one person. To tackle these decisively, public organizations are looking for new approaches. Design thinking offers an inviting perspective.

↪ That said, a thorough design-thinking process is hard to realize in a traditionally managed system. In that case, the danger of jumping to solutions looms large.

↪ The more experience of collaborations between designers and public organizations there are, the smoother these coalitions will go. But for the time being, mutual unfamiliarity with methodology, tools and mentality often stands in the way of an impactful collaboration.

↪ As such, creating a design space in (the primary processes of) public organizations deserves the fullest attention in a design-thinking process.

↪ It's important to understand which issues can benefit from a design thinking approach and in what way design thinking differs from the traditional approaches to these issues. The next few chapters will discuss these differences and how these can be put to good use.

Chapter 2

Design Thinking and Change Management

Public organizations prefer to tackle issues by using a rational process to select the best solution and then taking a systematic approach to achieve that solution. To achieve this can require negotiating on the solution to generate enough support and free up resources. This is the predominant approach to affecting change at public organizations. For wicked problems, however, further analysis and more negotiation don't work. Instead, taking a co-creative and learning approach to change offers more promise. Design thinking is one example of this type of approach. This chapter discusses change management insights in relation to design thinking, illustrating this connection with a case study on the closure of a number of bike tunnels in the Amsterdam region.

THE BEST DETOUR
OF THE NETHERLANDS

The A6 motorway that runs through the Amsterdam metropolitan area was being widened. For that to happen, a number of bike tunnels had to be temporarily closed. These types of closures are not unusual and in most cases they cause very few issues. In this case, however, the tunnels connected residential areas with schools and offices. As such, the tunnels played a very important role in the daily lives of the local population. What's more, several underpasses would be closed simultaneously and for a longer period of time. It's important to note here that cycling is one of the most important modes of transport in the Netherlands.

The contractor, who'd been employed by the state, assumed the state had made proper agreements with the municipality about these closures. Unfortunately, these agreements were open to interpretation and ultimately created an impasse when the municipality refused to issue a permit for the closures as long as there was no proper alternative for the cyclists. Although the municipality was not the one responsible for the detour, it was concerned that residents would hold it accountable.

The contractor had a vested interest in the permits being issued as quickly as possible, as any delays could lead to high costs. The state sympathized with both parties and also had a vested interest in emerging from the impasse with favourable, i.e. socially acceptable, costs.

Once it was clear there was no simple solution, the fine print of the contracts between the state, contractor and municipality was examined, followed by a series of meetings that didn't amount to much. Taking the standard approach to problem-solving in the public sector, i.e. collecting the facts (e.g. what's the problem, what's been discussed and are there alternative solutions?) and negotiating (e.g. are the possible solutions acceptable and who's going to pay for these?) no longer provided the answer. Things came to a standstill when no agreement could be reached on how much time was acceptable for a detour for cyclists. As the deadline approached, I was asked by the project manager if I could come up with anything that would break the impasse.

Fig. 4: Road signs for the detour. 'Omweg' is the Dutch word for 'detour'.

FIVE PREDOMINANT STYLES
OF CHANGE MANAGEMENT

How do you get an individual, an organization or even an entire sector on the side that leads to the desired change? What do you need to achieve this? Is it about system change, organizational change, a change in behaviour or a combination of all three? There are countless approaches to affecting change. Hans Vermaak and Leon de Caluwé, two leading change management experts, have clustered these into five styles of change management[15]. Their meta-theory has developed into a key standard in change management and also helps to better understand design thinking as an approach to change. The authors never reflected at length on design thinking as an approach to change. As such, this chapter supplements Vermaak and De Caluwé's meta-theory in part with my own experiences.

1.   The first style of change management concerns negotiating. Things change when you can align everyone's interests and reach a consensus through a negotiating process. This is also a game of power. This style is very evident in a political-management context. This style of change management has a very bad reputation[16]. Making decisions and creating policy becomes less about the content and more about power: how do you put the other party into checkmate? But that picture isn't entirely fair. Negotiating is based on a sound ideal, namely that people (always) see overarching interests and aim to realize shared effects. This ideal posits that people want to and can agree.

2.   The second style of change management concerns empirical understanding. This is a cognitive approach, with proposals developed based on objective, verifiable knowledge. Things change when you investigate what the best solution is and then systematically implement it in a rational process. Both the development and the implementation of proposals are done systematically with a firm belief in makeability and

planability. SMART goals are formulated, i.e. goals that are specific, measurable, achievable, realistic and time-bound. Engineers are major exponents of this style of change management, and thankfully so because you don't want there to be negotiations on how a building is going to be constructed. Policymakers generally also take a cognitive approach to change.

3.   Change can also come about by placing people in a learning situation and making them more aware and more capable through a development process, as a result of which their abilities increase. The third style of change management places learning centre stage. This helps those involved to look at an issue in a new way, to reach solutions in a process of co-creation and to examine their own perspective on how to do things. Designers prefer this style of change management—possibly supplemented with elements of the organic preferred style, as outlined in the last point[17]. Other examples of this style of change management are apprenticeships and game simulations.

4.   The fourth style of change management focuses on motivating people. When you stimulate people in the right way, they feel valued and seen in a social process, thereby facilitating change. This is about loyalty and quid pro quos. It's also about a sense of community, involvement and attention for others. This style of change management is typical of HR managers for instance.

5.   The fifth style of change management is organic in nature and is about giving meaning. Those using this style focus on patterns in organizations: why is something happening the way it's happening? Change will happen organically if obstacles impeding a dynamic process are removed. Unlike the other four styles, this style of change management is far less associated with a particular group of people in a particular place.

You see this style in many places in organizations. Even people with another predominant style of change management—in particular designers with a learning style of change management—use organic change to support their approach.

The five styles of change management each have their own traits, forms and language, as outlined in figure 6[18].

WHAT'S THE BEST STYLE OF CHANGE MANAGEMENT?

An important note to make regarding styles of change management is that although they may be fundamentally different, there's no hierarchy. Which style will deliver the best result depends on the situation. In other words, it depends on the issue in question. Chapter 1 outlined various types of issues using Arno Koster's classification and the following section will link this classification (see figure 2) to the effective styles of change management.

First, there are the simple issues in the first quadrant according to Koster's classification—these are not in the scope of this book. If everyone simply does their work, these issues will be resolved. Then there are the issues that require more knowledge. In this case, the preferred option is the cognitive style of change management. For ethical or ideological issues, i.e. where there's plenty of knowledge, but no consensus, it's the negotiating repertoire that dominates. These issues will also not be discussed.

This book is about wicked problems: the (social) issues that no one entirely understands and that cannot be effectively addressed by any one person. These are the issues where more analysis and further negotiation no longer provide a solution.

A second important note to make is that the first two styles of change management mentioned dominate in public

Fig. 6:   Five styles of change.

	NEGOTIATION (Power)	EMPIRICAL UNDER-STANDING (Cognitive)
THINGS CHANGE WHEN YOU	align interests	first think and then do things systematically
THIS HAPPENS IN A	game of power	rational process
TOWARDS	a feasible solution, win/win	the best solution in a makeable world
INTERVENTIONS INCLUDE	forming coalitions, top structuring	project-based working, strategic analysis
THROUGH A	process director who uses their authority	content expert, project leader
FOCUSSED ON	positions and context	knowledge and results
THE RESULT IS	unknown and shifting	defined and guaranteed
THE GUARANTEE IS IN	policy documents, power balance, loyalty	measuring = knowing and adjusting
THE PITFALLS ARE IN	flights of fancy, lose/lose	ignoring external or irrational aspects
TYPICAL ACTORS INCLUDE	in addition to the process director: people with most formal or informal power, representatives of interests, grassroots supporters, 'bystanders' and the surrounding environment	in addition to the process leader/expert: clients, project staff, target groups, end-users and the (angry) outside world

FIVE STYLES OF CHANGE

LEARNING	MOTIVATING	ORGANIC
introduce people to a learning situation	stimulate people in the right way	make space for spontaneous evolution
development process	trading exercises	dynamic process
a solution reached through co-creation	a motivating solution, the 'best fit'	a solution that releases energy
reframing the issue, empathic research, prototyping	assessing and rewarding, social meetings	open space meetings, self-learning teams
designer or context builder (process leader)	HRM expert, a coaching manager	pattern identifier who puts themself in the game
shared meaning, setting and communication	procedures, inspiration, atmosphere	complexity and meanings
unknown and often lies outside the original scope	conceived, not guaranteed	unpredictable
the connection that end-user has with the process and follow-up outcomes	HRM system, good relationships, communication	self-organization, quality of the dialogue
ignoring content or systematic complexity, (endless) analysis without taking any action	suffocating systems, soft healers	complexity not being thought through fully, muddling through within the wrong frame
in addition to the designer and the process director: end-users and specialists from the organizations involved	in addition to the HRM expert/manager: the tastemakers, HR staff, team builders, role models and stakeholders	in addition to the pattern identifier: intrapreneurs and entrepreneurs, everyone who takes the initiative, sponsors and innovators, networks

organizations: the cognitive style of change management that's based on a process of empirical understanding and the style of change management based on negotiating. These styles are effective in ethical and scientific/expert issues as mentioned in Koster's classification.

In the case of wicked problems, the predominant styles of change management are often not enough. Another approach, however, is design thinking. This approach is a learning style of change management, but also draws on the organic style of change management where giving meaning is paramount. In general, public organizations have far less experience with these styles of change management and if they do, it's often not very positive. Arno Koster's classification helps to recognize wicked problems and opens up the need to discuss a new approach.

To successfully apply design thinking, it's important to properly understand how people who use the predominant styles of change management will react to it and how design thinking can be complementary to other styles of change management. After all—and this is the third important note to make—with wicked problems, you have to be able to draw on several resources, i.e. be able to apply several styles of change management at the same time. This is certainly no easy task because different styles of change management can really clash.

The rest of this chapter will focus on design thinking in relation to the two styles of change management that dominate at public organizations, i.e. negotiating and empirical understanding, because this relationship is often crucial to the success of the design process.

Innovation
is rarely the
result of
predictability.

THE BEST DETOUR
OF THE NETHERLANDS

We proposed postponing the negotiations about the closure of the tunnels and instead to start talking with the users of the tunnels to see what the closure means to them. They'd been overlooked a little in the process, as a result of which our suggestion was embraced. We were tasked with finding an acceptable solution. The fact that everyone was happy the endless meetings would end undoubtedly also played a role in us getting the job.

But we didn't immediately start on a design process. We first conducted a few analyses and interventions in line with other change management strategies.

To begin with, we carried out a negotiation analysis: who'd actually be deciding whether the proposal we'd develop would be acceptable, and on what grounds? We concluded that the client, i.e. Rijkswaterstaat (the executive agency of the Ministry of Infrastructure and Water Management), would find the proposal acceptable if the intended result, i.e. preventing the delay of the construction process, was achieved against socially acceptable costs.

The contractor would find nearly every proposal that prevented a delay acceptable and the municipality would find nearly every proposal on the closure acceptable as long as it had the community's support.

We followed this analysis with a systematic analysis – in line with the cognitive style of change management – of the critical path: how much time did we actually have to put forward a solution? That proved a tough task. The schedule of work for this big project was difficult to read and even more difficult to interpret. Working with the project controls manager, we deduced what the critical deadline would be to still be able to prevent a delay and also which important milestones preceded this and how much leeway there was with them.

The intervention that we'd intended to take as part of this, and that we unfortunately forgot about, was sharing the work schedule with all of the stakeholders – something we regretted doing later in the process.

One intervention that is part of a cognitive approach that we did do, however, is to agree a work budget with the state that would cover our solution. Designers sometimes understandably tend to want to leave this open because you have no idea at the start of a project what the final proposal will entail. But because we had no idea what amount the client deemed as 'socially acceptable', we decided to agree this immediately.

We were nearly ready to start, but one thing still had to be sorted, namely that our proposal might be noticeably different than what had been imagined up to now. In this case, we carried out an intervention in line with the negotiating style of change management and agreed with the parties involved that our solution didn't have to be about the detour time per se — something that had been the entire focus of the discussion up to then. This was important because we already felt that the framing of the situation, i.e. that inconvenience = detour time, had made the problem unsolvable.

FRIENDLY FIRE

Even though designers and public sector staff tend to welcome each other with open arms, they can both experience a lot of unexpected resistance. This is because of a certain paradox: although all parties are open to working together and designers gain explicit trust, the core of the public organizations in question has a near-allergic reaction to the design approach. Embracing a new style of change management doesn't mean that the predominant styles of change management are rendered obsolete. In fact, the values and opinions that are part of the predominant styles of change management will clash a lot with the values and opinions anchored in design thinking.

There are tensions, which if left neglected, will lead to friendly fire, i.e. an affable form of resistance that can weaken a successful design process. Friendly fire can be predicted, explained and avoided if you identify the tensions between the different styles of change management in good time.

FRIENDLY FIRE: WHEN DESIGN THINKING MEETS EMPIRICAL UNDERSTANDING

When applying a design approach at a public organization, one of the key tensions is the clash with the change management style of empirical understanding. This tension arises because public organizations have to be accountable for the decisions they make and the money they spend. This leads to core values like working systematically and being goal-oriented and first time right. Terms such as objectivity, evaluation, modelling and avoiding risk are part and parcel of this. These values are almost the polar opposite to a design approach, which instead places a combination of thinking and doing, iterating and not knowing centre stage. In the case of design thinking, the key concepts are subjectivity, interpretation and experience.

These tensions can lead to a situation where proponents of a cognitive style of change management lose confidence in the process, while designers get the feeling that everything is on the right track. Friendly fire arises then from those proponents of a cognitive style of change management trying to stop the design-thinking process, e.g. by using pocket vetoes or by simply starting an alternative process and letting the design process peter out. Friendly fire from designers is expressed by them retreating or overwhelming proponents of a cognitive style of change management with insights and proposals at a certain stage. They then, in turn, have no idea how the final proposal was reached and will exhibit friendly fire once the proposal is on the table. At this point, support and objectivity will be cast in doubt, prompting a discussion of whether the proposal will work at all.

Thankfully, partnerships between designers and proponents of a cognitive style of change management often go well. But this requires such things as designers being introduced properly and proponents of a cognitive style of change management continuing to see how they—the designers—contribute to the process that leads to a good proposal. In thorough design processes like frame innovation (see page 32), the

Fig. 7: When design thinking meets empirical understanding.

WHEN DESIGN THINKING MEETS EMPIRICAL UNDERSTANDING

QUESTIONS THAT ARE PART OF A COGNITIVE STYLE OF CHANGE MANAGEMENT	ANSWERS THAT DESIGNERS GIVE
What expectations are we creating if we speak to end-users? *Proponents of a cognitive style of change management prefer to talk about a concrete issue, with a clear agenda.*	If you're genuinely interested, then you won't create any (false) expectations. *A designer often has no idea yet what they're going to discover, let alone what question or observation is going to lead to that insight.*
How do we know if we've spoken to enough people? *Proponents of a cognitive style of change management are guided by statistics, the ability to model situations and falsifiability. 'Support' is (more or less) quantifiable.*	If we're not getting any further information from speaking to people and have found our angle, then we've spoken to enough people. *Designers are guided by interpretation, their own fascination and the situation. Determining whether there's enough support is often an intuitive thing.*
Are we in control? *A cognitive approach does well in a planned and controlled environment.*	We know where the uncertainties are and will investigate these. *Innovation is rarely the result of predictability.*
What will it deliver? *Proponents of a cognitive style of change management appreciate efficiency and having a goal. First, they decide what the answer should be and then they work towards this in a systematic fashion.*	If we knew that, then we wouldn't need to make it anymore. *Designers combine thinking and doing. Relatively speaking, they spend a lot of time on understanding the problem and less time on the solution.*

archaeology step, for instance, provides the opportunity for a discussion on why more of the same, i.e. empirical understanding and negotiation, will no longer work (see also section 6.1). Proponents of a cognitive style of change management are also included in the design process because there's clearly room for factual knowledge and expert judgement.

FRIENDLY FIRE: WHEN DESIGN THINKING
                          MEETS NEGOTIATING

The rules of the game in the world of negotiating are very different to those in the world of design (see figure 8). In the case of design, openness about what you want to learn is important. You state what your limitations are in terms of knowledge and abilities. You ask for help and you experiment, the aim of which is to do better. In the case of negotiating, a lot of what you know is kept hidden and close to your chest. Crucial conversations are conducted behind closed doors.

Another tension is caused by the fact that the negotiating world makes clear who the important players are and at whose negotiating table the discussions will take place. A design approach starts with the end-user, often revealing that a person or party is less important than was previously thought. In particular, parties who say they're speaking on behalf of other parties often ultimately prove to have far less of a mandate than had been accepted. This also means that new parties are important for the support of proposals: parties that are—consciously or not—ignored by the negotiating world.

One final tension between a design approach and a negotiating one is that directors of public organizations can be held accountable for the measures taken. They become vulnerable if proposals are not politically feasible, cannot be implemented, do not (immediately) have the desired effect or if the wrong perception is created (more of which in sections 6.3 and 6.4).

The tensions between design thinking and negotiating nearly always arise. Whether they build to friendly fire depends on

Political ideology is often just an excuse to not have to think any further.

Professor Thomas Fisher

the extent to which the proponents of a negotiating style of change management focus on power and the extent to which designers are sensitive to the complexities of (politics and) governance. A typical response from a negotiator is that they want to retreat to ideological isolation instead of showing any vulnerability. Or as Professor Thomas Fisher[19] laments: "Political ideology is often just an excuse to not have to think any further." The most prevalent friendly fire from designers is ignoring or simply denying power structures. That said, I do also see designers raising the white flag and admitting that they're just not strategic enough.

Thankfully, there are plenty of examples of things going well. For instance, one director once gave us the amazingly simply instruction: "Surprise me, but don't take me by surprise." That's an easy rule of the game that can provide a solid foundation for a successful partnership between a designer and a negotiator. I'm also meeting more and more designers who want to know how a decision-making process is organized.

FRIENDLY FIRE: WHEN COGNITIVE
                  MEETS NEGOTIATING

It's not only design thinking that can lead to friendly fire; tensions can also arise between proponents of a cognitive style of change management who base their actions on empirical understanding and those with a negotiating style. These may be the predominant styles of change management at public organizations, but those with more experience will be familiar with the phenomenon of a carefully realized bureaucratic proposal not being supported by the board. That may be because a director wants to see proposals within a certain timeframe that doesn't give the bureaucrats enough time to gather any new insights, and make any proposals therefore. Listen to the water cooler conversations at public organizations and you'll soon get a good idea of the situations that this creates.

In most cases, ways of working have been found to ease the tensions between these styles of change management. For instance, by setting up line management differently, namely

Fig. 8:   When design thinking meets negotiating.

WHEN DESIGN THINKING MEETS NEGOTIATING

QUESTIONS THAT ARE PART OF A NEGOTIATING STYLE OF CHANGE MANAGEMENT	ANSWERS THAT DESIGNERS GIVE
Did you speak to the right people? *With the 'right people', negotiators primarily mean stakeholders with power.*	We've spoken to and observed the right people. *Designers think about the end-users in the first place.*
Is it a (politically) feasible pro-posal? *The decision-making process is often predictable. But sometimes it's (seemingly) a lottery. For instance, cases that have noth-ing to do with each other in terms of gaining support are sudden-ly linked. As such, decisions are preferably 'precooked', making the process merely a formality.*	Let's hear what others have to say about it. *Designers assume openness and vul-nerability, and as such introduce uncertainty in the negotiating pro-cess. Because there's no consider-ation for such things like a hidden agenda, the decision-making process becomes unpredictable.*
Can I sell this? *Negotiators reach a result in a world that is permanently 'unsafe' (see also section 6.4). Both political opponents and the media have a vested interest in conflict.*	We'll have to find out if it works while doing it. *Designers assume a safe environ-ment where mistakes can be made and repeat iterations can be conducted. If the environment appears unsafe however, they can get defensive and the process become vulnerable.*

more senior management linking empirical understanding and negotiating. Content-based proposals are tested at this level in terms of 'sensitivity to the complexities of (politics and) governance' and 'political desirability and feasibility'. There are very few established ways of working between a negotiating approach and a design-thinking one, and cognitive change and design thinking. This, too, is a job for the process leader of design thinking.

A BETTER UNDERSTANDING OF HOW DIFFERENT STYLES OF CHANGE MANAGEMENT INTERACT

This chapter outlines how design thinking works as a learning style of change management, supported by an organic style of change management. It then compares design thinking with the characteristics of the two other styles of change management that dominate the public sector: negotiation and empirical understanding. These styles are like different planets spinning in the same universe. The figure on pages 46 and 47 presents their fundamental differences.

THE BEST DETOUR OF THE NETHERLANDS

Fig. 9

Road sign for the detour. This sign doesn't tell you how much longer your journey will be because of the detour or how much more time you'll spend travelling; it tells you how many calories you'll lose.

We encountered friendly fire a number of times when dealing with the issue of bike tunnel closures in the Amsterdam area, primarily between proponents of a cognitive style of change management and designers. We were also able to avoid it a number of times.

Our field research with the users of the tunnels resulted in two key insights. The first was that for most people the detour time was not such an important point; instead there were greater concerns about the social and physical safety. That's understandable because the detour went past the building site and also through a poorly lit park. These facts made most users worry about the safety of their children. Armed with these insights, we approached the aldermen in charge. We told them about the process and the insights, and said that we'd shortly be conducting design sessions with the youngsters to optimize the route of the detour in terms of social and physical safety. To underline that we were setting the bar high, we unveiled a board with the street name 'The Best Detour of the Netherlands'.

The aldermen were enthusiastic about the reframing; it eradicated the sense that a proper closure primarily depended on the detour time. The aldermen asked us to flesh out some things and present a more detailed plan two weeks later. They wanted to have an idea of the measures the design sessions might produce. What's more, they wanted additional assurance that we'd be able to reach enough people during the summer period — the period in which this issue arose — to ensure community support.

We were very happy with the discussions. After all, one of the most important steps of the design process had been taken. We'd introduced a new way of looking at things that people went along with and that offered a lot of perspective. As such, we were incredibly surprised to learn the very next day from our client at Rijkswaterstaat that they'd concluded our attempts had failed.

It took a while before it was clear to us what was going on. It'd been assumed that we'd present our proposals and that the municipality would give a go/no-go sign. This expectation is very much in line with an organization where the predominant styles of change management are founded on negotiating and empirical understanding: you analyze, make a proposal and ensure agreement. The people at the ministry didn't understand our design-thinking process explanation that we were not far along enough in our design process yet to have concrete proposals. "Why," they asked, "did you then go to the aldermen?"

Looking back, we should have better informed the organizations involved of the nature of a design process. We should have made it more widely known that our presentation was a step in the process, the aim of which was to assess the feasibility of the new frame; it was not intended to be used to reach a compromise. In retrospect, we would have done ourselves a favour had we shared the schedule we were aiming for at the start of the process with all the stakeholders. By neglecting the right interventions that support the design process, we got caught in some friendly fire.

Fig. 10: The dominant approaches to change compared to design thinking

60

THREE APPROACHES TO TACKLING PROBLEMS

	NEGOTIATION (Power)	EMPIRICAL UNDERSTANDING (Cognitive)	DESIGN THINKING
ROOT	Ideology	Logic	Aesthetics
BASIC STANCE	Wanting (ethical)	Thinking (intellectual)	Feeling (empathetic)
CORE VALUE	Intersubjective	Objective	Subjective
EXPLANATION	Argumentation	Evaluation	Interpretation
STARTING POINT	Conflict (urgency)	Definition (curiosity)	Illustration (engagement)
RELATION TO SUBJECT	Influence	Distance	Participation
AUTHORITY DUE TO ABILITY TO	Connect	Explain	Inspire
RESULT	Agreement	Model	New Meaning

We were very vulnerable at this point in the process. However, by having a lot of meetings in a short space of time and appeasing everyone, we ensured the old negotiations and unfeasible proposals didn't end up back on the table. We survived this because we had a good understanding of what we were doing, the stakeholders didn't have a plan B, our contact person at Rijkswaterstaat was overseeing the process and could assuage others, and – possibly most importantly of all – everyone really wanted a solution. Two weeks later, we were able to present out solution.

The fundamental differences between the styles of change management can create tension and lead to friendly fire, which is something you want to avoid. However, you can't do this by simply choosing one style of change management over the other. On the contrary, wicked problems require a synergy between the different styles of change management. For instance, allowing uncertainty, i.e. a learning capacity, will facilitate another way of thinking and also create an openness to the relational, so that that the task in hand can be completed together[20].

It's often a good idea for wicked problems to have design thinking act as the leading approach, with the two predominant styles, i.e. negotiating and empirical understanding,—logically—fulfilling a support role. As we're dealing with an issue that can't be isolated from the environment in which it exists, designers can't retreat to an island and then present a final proposal at the end. Solutions can only be reached by working with and within public organizations.

Surprise me, but don't take me by surprise.

Instruction by a public sector
director to my team.

THE BEST DETOUR
OF THE NETHERLANDS

All parties appointed representatives who were to help us where necessary. Each was an expert in their field and open to a design approach, and ultimately made an important contribution in the search for a solution. We involved these representatives in every step along the way: the field-work, the co-creative design process, the implementation and the ceremonial opening of the detour.

For instance, two traffic experts worked with residents on the final route for the detour. They'd already created a detour based, as is standard practice, on the shortest possible detour time. This detour met all protocols and guidelines. However, once it became clear that safety was more important to residents than the detour time, the traffic experts set aside their first proposal instead of defending it. Under our supervision, they initiated a co-creative process with the residents, with each party taking the other seriously. As a result, the final route of the detour was decided pretty quickly.

The state installed lighting along the detour that had been decided with the residents. The municipality also decided to cut back the hedging along the detour earlier than planned, so that there was a clearer view. The municipality also decided to include the detour in its road de-icing schedule: in the case of freezing weather, the path would remain accessible.

Working together with students from a local secondary school, we drafted the communication on the tunnel closures. Among other things, the students took care of the signage to guide people safely from A to B. Using the building signs, they also shared their surprising, sometimes slightly confusing and also funny thoughts on the large building project (see figures 4, 5 and 9). Photos of the signs went viral – even the Dutch Minister of Infrastructure and Water Management tweeted about them – which led to the residents being much better informed than usual about the building work. A positive side effect was that more people visited the detour to look at and photograph the signs. This additional stream of people created an even greater sense of safety.

The residents were satisfied, as evident from statements they made ("This is better than the bike routes we had") and the municipality's request to maintain the detour as a full-time connection after the bicycle tunnels reopened. When wrapping up the project, one of the aldermen referred to the Best Detour of the Netherlands as an example of a successful coalition between all parties.

Key Ideas in This Chapter

↳   There are five dominant styles of change management recognized in this field of study. These are based, respectively, on negotiating (power), empirical understanding (cognitive), learning, motivation and an organic process to break down barriers. Design thinking is part of the learning style, using for support the organic style of change management that places meaning centre stage.

↳   As a rule, negotiating and empirical understanding are the predominant styles of change management at public organizations.

↳   Although design thinking may cover part of the change management repertoire, what it covers is precisely what public organizations are less confident in and which wicked problems need a lot of.

↳   In the case of wicked problems, a design process cannot develop separately from the context in which the problem exists. This means that a design approach will always have to seek a synergy with (in particular) the cognitive and thenegotiating styles of change management.

↳   Different styles of change management can clash.
       Even if there's a desire to work together, friendly fire
       may arise between the different agents of change.

↳   Ways of working have been found to deal with the
       tensions between the negotiation and empirical under-
       standing styles of change management at public
       organizations and to avoid or resist friendly fire. There
       are no such ways of working for the tensions between
       a design-thinking approach and the negotiation and
       empirical understanding styles of change management.
       As such, the process leader is responsible for the
       important task of avoiding friendly fire.

Chapter 3

Design Thinking and Coalition Roles

Chapter 2 showed that public organizations prefer to deal with issues using styles of change management based on rational processes and negotiation. In the case of wicked problems however, an exploratory learning approach offers more promise. This requires a specific form of collaboration between the parties involved, one that designers can help develop. Chapter 3 addresses the different roles that public sector staff can play in coalitions and what design thinking can contribute. A case study on the introduction of the Netherlands' Social Support Act (Wet maatschappelijke ondersteuning, Wmo) illustrates this.

With wicked problems, nobody's in charge. As such, no person or organization can take a directive role in a coalition.

The difficulties parties experience when collaborating often hinder the search for a solution. There can be dozens of reasons why a coalition between different parties doesn't have the desired dynamic or isn't delivering the desired result. For instance, those involved may have strong, differing characters or conflicting opinions. One of the parties may not have enough knowledge or may have a hidden agenda. But even if this isn't the case and everyone is competent and has good intentions, a coalition can still experience some ugly hiccups. This can happen if someone takes on a role that isn't in line with what the coalition aims to achieve.

My outline of the roles in different types of coalition is again based on a meta-theory, namely the 'spectrum of forming a coalition' devised by Martine de Jong[21]. This spectrum defines three roles that a public organization can play: a directing role, a partnering role and a facilitating role. None of these roles is better than the other per se and each situation will dictate which role is the most suitable. These roles are very different however. The behaviour and types of coalition of one role are unsuitable for another. Recognizing and discussing these roles helps to properly position a design approach.

CASE STUDY PART 1

SOCIAL SUPPORT ACT

Legislation regarding long-term care in the Netherlands was reformed in 2015 and laid down in the Social Support Act (Wet maatschappelijke ondersteuning, Wmo). With this act, the quality of social support was adapted to be more in line with society's changing needs. People want to be able to live at home for as long as possible, keep control of their own lives and not be lonely. The government wants to offer suitable support in people's living environments and wants social networks and community facilities to supplement each other as much as possible. When the Wmo was introduced, responsibility for its implementation was also decentralized from the state to the municipalities. They were tasked with boosting accessibility to facilities, services and spaces for people with a disability.

This decentralisation was a major task for municipalities, which up until then hadn't had to deal with this issue on such a scale. Where would they get the expertise for this so quickly to be able to steer things properly? Where to start?

In this case, Twynstra Gudde[22] was asked by a municipality to bring together a group of professional parties to work on a process. The task was to gather input for the community policy in the form of a manifesto. What the municipality in fact wanted was to investigate how it could fulfil a directing role.

THE PUBLIC ORGANIZATION IN A DIRECTING ROLE

If a public organization has a clear ambition that it wants to realize with others, then it takes on a directing role because it initiated the process. They steer this process towards a concrete result and take a directive approach. The initiating party's ambition determines which parties are invited to collaborate. This coalition is usually formal in structure, e.g. weekly project meetings, open consultation evenings or sounding boards.

In this type of coalition, the formal world of procedures plays the leading role as opposed to the informal world of relationships. A directive approach is a very suitable approach for forcing things. Take the persistent problem of littering, for instance. The government can decide to introduce a deposit on cans and small PET bottles, knowing that this is an effective measure. Ownership in this form of coalition is not shared and the initiating party weighs up the stakeholders' differing interests. As such, before moving to a deposit scheme, the costs that the packaging industry and the retailers will have to incur for a collection system are weighed up against the social benefit of less litter.

On the one hand, progress in this type of coalition is based on a project-oriented approach. The intended solution is determined from the outset and a process is developed that makes clear how every step will lead to the end result. On the other hand, this is combined with a negotiation approach because the stakeholders, who often don't have any immediate vested interest in the intended solution, will do everything they can to ensure their interests are showcased as much as possible. That's how the packaging industry and its effective lobby have been able to prevent the introduction of a deposit on cans and small PET bottles in the Netherlands for years.

THE PUBLIC ORGANIZATION IN A PARTNERING ROLE

If there are several parties that will each contribute to and gain something from a common stated ambition, then the parties play a partnering role. This type of coalition is suitable when none of the parties is calling the shots and each of the parties depends on the other to achieve their shared goals. The primary directive in this type of coalition is more about achieving goals and less about a concrete result. This type of coalition takes a collective approach.

A good example of this is municipalities that make agreements together about the distribution of facilities. Not every municipality can be home to a swimming pool or theatre, but together they can organize this at a regional level. This requires distribution of facilities and a collective investment in their accessibility. The objective is to be able to offer a good level of facilities.

Typical forms in this type of coalition are steering committees on which each party has a seat, team day trips and team-building sessions, and vision-forming processes. The parties

We had to come up with a brilliant solution, but were in no way meant to set up a co-creative process for that.

participate fully in the coalition, each fulfilling their own role and contributing to the common objective. The change management repertoire used is not as clearly outlined as with a directing role. However, a lot of the progress comes from the project-oriented approach in which shared ambitions are translated into goals, usually along with a schedule and budget. With a partnering role, negotiations still have to be conducted, e.g. on (relinquishing) authority, the formulation of the shared ambition and contribution of required resources. That said, the negotiating game doesn't set the tone as much as it does in a directive coalition with a single directing party.

CASE STUDY PART 2

SOCIAL SUPPORT ACT

To be able to implement the Wmo requires an active collaboration with medical insurers, healthcare providers and other stakeholders in neighbourhoods, districts and villages, like general practitioners. These professionals are clearly very experienced when it comes to long-term care. As such, the municipality decided to go looking in its own city for partners who wanted to give their input on how to fulfil the Wmo policy. This included volunteers and volunteering organizations, social entrepreneurs, healthcare organizations and, of course, clients.

The design team set up an open co-creative process. As a result, the directing relationship quickly became a point of discussion between the municipality and the intended partners. A concise manifesto, like the one the municipality had proposed with a sort of menu stating what was expected of the municipality, was not what the parties could or wanted to make. They were more focussed on the question of how they were all going to work together in this city.

The parties agreed on the shared ambition to have healthcare and wellbeing align more with the needs and experiences of the clients and their environment. This mainly comprised several further questions: How will we support each other? How will we work together? How will we ensure that it's always clear why we're doing what we're doing? These questions were also shared by the civil servants responsible at the municipality.

THE PUBLIC ORGANIZATION
IN A FACILITATING ROLE

The third coalition role is that of facilitator. This role is suitable if results or goals are not being forced and as such it's ideal for wicked problems in particular—these are (social) issues that no one entirely understands and that cannot be effectively addressed by any one person. In this case, a connective approach is taken.

Both the institutional stakeholders and the end-users are challenged to start a movement based on their own personal motivations that will contribute to solving the wicked problem. This is best achieved with a connective ambition at the heart of the movement. In other words, if everyone can use their own motivations to contribute to a higher-level shared ambition. This coalition is based on the right conditions to facilitate change.

A good example in this case is the coalition between the government, housing associations and the refugee network that aims to find accommodation for people with a residence permit. A place can be made in this coalition for status holders, i.e. refugees who have been granted asylum status, but it cannot force them to feel at home. Or take the central case study in chapter 2: the government and the contractor can ensure that a detour is safe according to all standards, but it cannot force users to also feel safe.

This connective type of coalition is typically characterized by closer and looser relationships that change in composition. Motivations in this type of coalition are more important than functions and positions. In such a setting, ideas, developments and movements can be created that had not been thought of previously and certainly weren't provided for.

This type of coalition requires a good process leader. They have to keep an eye out for non-committal involvement and ensure that people continue to feel a connection. If they don't, then people will easily leave the coalition and head down another path.

The process leader also plays an important role in developing and monitoring the connective ambition. This ambition is not set in stone, but does offer an important constant touchstone. For instance, do the initiatives really contribute to the connective ambition? If so, then the public organization can be called on for support. Facilitating can be done with policy and policy instruments (like money), but also by using a support resource, e.g. a subject specialist from the government who helps look at the feasibility of the ideas. Facilitating can also be achieved through contacts and focus, two points that chapter 5 will return to.

DESIGNING THE COALITION

It's important that public sector staff are aware of their role in a coalition: a directing role, a partnering role or a facilitating one. They should also be aware of what type of coalition is suitable and how this can be organized. Other questions that may be raised include: How do we want to relate to each other? What do we need for that? Therefore, it's also important to know whether the coalition is based on achieving a result, goal or movement. If this is uncertain, it may lead to an uncertainty about how to fill the roles.

I've made the mistake more than once of setting to work with my team all too cheerfully after being hired to solve a wicked problem in a creative fashion. With the motto "Everyone who's part of the problem must be able to be part of the solution", we set off into the world. This led to huge confusion among all the parties involved who didn't appear to understand what we came to do. We were quickly put 'under observation' by the organization that had hired us. We had to come up with a brilliant solution, but we were in no way meant to set up a co-creative process for that. Instead of being free to build on working relationships with all parties, we now had to ask the project leader for permission for every meeting with an outside party. This created resistance because we wanted the organization that had hired us to play a facilitating role. The organization, however, wanted to retain a directing role. It was only when we understood this and discussed that the current type of coalition was in part sustaining the problem, that the space was created to develop a new type of coalition.

Figure 11 lists a few of the typical characteristics concerning the different types of coalitions.

THE COALITION AGENTS
AT PUBLIC ORGANIZATIONS

Regardless of which coalition role is the most suitable—directing, partnering or facilitating—public sector staff working on the boundary between their organization and the outside world of the end-users embody this role. These people are also referred to as 'boundary spanners'. Typical boundary spanners are stakeholder managers, alliance managers, participation managers, community workers, youth workers, etc.

Boundary spanners are the first to see when a coalition role is not working (or no longer working) and that another role should be taken. Just like an expert in change management can switch between the five styles of change management, a boundary spanner is like a coalition specialist who can switch between the three different coalition roles. Chapter 4 is all about what boundary spanners do in practice.

DESIGN THINKING AS
A CONNECTIVE REPERTOIRE

A connective way of working with the public organization in the facilitating role offers the most promise when dealing with wicked problems. To find a solution, all stakeholders must be able to be a part of the process. This is best achieved if people are encouraged to contribute based on their own motivations. A facilitating role can lead to meaningful results, but the path to achieving this is uncertain. The direction this type of coalition takes cannot be predetermined nor can the results

Fig. 11: Characteristics of different roles in coalitions.

CHARACTERISTICS OF DIFFERENT ROLES IN COALITIONS

ROLE	DIRECTING	PARTNERING	FACILITATING
APPROACH	Initiating party's ambition leads the way	Collective Ambition	Motivations of all stakeholders as cornerstone for connective ambition
PROCES SUPERVISION AIMED AT	Moving parties to make the necessary contribution to realize the ambition	The parties involved endorsing the shared ambition and pursuing obligations to acquire the necessary resources	Developing a connective ambition based on the stakeholders' motivations that gives all stakeholders the space to contribute on their own terms
LANGUAGE	Mandate, position, support, authority, framework, guidelines, alignment, decision-making and implementation	Commitment, relationships, rules of the game, trust, alliance, cooperation and shared responsibility	Bottom-up, local, participation, energy, hospitality, movement, inspiration, sharing, meeting, ownership and community

You can't expect
a process
facilitator
to steer the
process to a
predetermined
result.

of this type of coalition, and this can make process leaders in a traditionally managed system feel very uneasy. Even experienced process leaders have to work out how to convince their own organization that this is the best role to take. A facilitating role presents the process leader with the question of how to connect the organization's in-house obligation to deliver results with the spontaneous effects outside the organization[23].

Design thinking is a very suitable and valuable approach to provide context for a connective way of working. Firstly, because the empathic research of design thinking is an excellent way to identify the motivations of the parties involved. This type of research reveals what motivates end-users and what holds them back. Section 6.2 will cover this in more detail. Secondly, because the shared ambition and a connective and inviting way of looking are important cornerstones of a thorough design process. In terms of design, I mean a shared view of the issue in question, i.e. a frame (see chapter 1).

Boundary spanners and designers seamlessly help each other to design a connective coalition. The boundary spanners first identify when the public organization needs to take a facilitating role. After all, the boundary spanners are connected to the systems of their own organization and can, therefore, safeguard progress of the process in the facilitating organizations.

CASE STUDY PART 3

SOCIAL SUPPORT ACT

When fleshing out the shared ambition, i.e. to have healthcare and well-being be more aligned with the needs and experiences of clients and their environment, the decision was made to choose a learning process that would connect different civil servants, professionals and volunteers for six months. Our design team supported this learning process.

Patients' stories helped steer the joint search for better healthcare and wellbeing in this municipality. One of the key themes to emerge from this was dependence. How could dependence be re-evaluated and new forms of dependence sought instead of focussing on independence? There were a number of paradoxes with this theme. In the words of one of the clients: "I want to decide for myself who I'm dependent on". As part of the search for a new perspective the film The Swedish Theory Of Love was shown to illustrate the downsides of a society that is designed to maximize independence.

The municipality didn't give a straight-forward and definitive answer to the initial question. Instead, something far more beautiful happened: the stakeholders in the community and the municipality inspired a joint movement. Together, they produced prototypes like 'Do-it-yourself daily activities' – a new way to spend the day in which the clients' experience takes centre stage – and 'Connecting with care' – an initiative to link healthcare and personal development. The stakeholders developed these and other initiatives further, under the banner of 'The Circle'.

The most important outcome from this process is quite possibly The Circle itself. On the basis of trust and shared responsibility, this growing network of professionals, civil servants, clients and volunteers helps shape and provide context for the future of healthcare and wellbeing in the city. The municipality facilitates the process through such things as get-togethers to flesh out and assess the prototypes and an online platform where the members of the network can meet.

THE POSITION OF THE DESIGNER IN THE COALITION

In most of the case studies in this book, designers have been contracted for a shorter or longer period of time to work with a public organization or on a joint venture. As such, they are not an independent player in the coalition, but fly the flag of the party they represent. This legitimizes their involvement.

That said, it's not essential per se for the designer to have a public organization as their client for a successful approach to a social issue. A designer can also operate independently on the playing field, in which case they are not a hired process leader, but rather an autonomous player using their own fascination and intrinsic motivations to get something moving.

A BROWNFIELD SITE

A few years ago, a group of designers got together under the leadership of Jan Boelen[24] in a Belgian town to discuss a brownfield site, i.e. a piece of land that was contaminated with heavy metals like led and zinc. The municipality had placed a fence around the contaminated site to keep people away from it and prevent any danger to public health. The wild terrain and the fence were an eyesore to the community.

The designers got in touch with a group of scientists and decided together to come up with a strategy to make the land usable again and give it back to the community. It emerged that plants could be used to decontaminate the soil, in which case the soil wouldn't have to be dug up and removed, and therefore would minimize the cost of decontamination. Although the process of decontamination would take seven years, the fence around the site could be taken down after the plants had been

planted because they'd hold on to the contaminated soil.

The neighbourhood community was involved in the plan through a social design process. The designers presented the options for decontaminating the soil using plants, adding that if the residents wanted to have the green space back again, then they'd be expected to spend seven years sowing and harvesting together.

Once the commitment for this was obtained, the designers set to work on the project with a critical, speculative design process. If you harvest the plants and press them in blocks to dry them, the led and zinc can be extracted from the plants depending on technological progress over the next 10-15 years. People can then earn money from this.

This project could be realized because the scientists had a research budget they wanted to invest in it and from which they could pay for the designers' involvement. The municipality only embraced the project when the designers could demonstrate they had a solid strategy that was supported by the neighbourhood. At that point, the government took a facilitating role, by organizing neighbourhood meetings, among other things.

The process of sowing and harvesting has already been ongoing for a number of years now.

Regardless of how a designer gets involved in a wicked problem— whether it's as a contractor or in an autonomous role—if a public organization is part of the problem, then it's very likely it will be asked to facilitate the process at a certain point. In its mildest form, this role will entail them agreeing with the activities. However, more often than not, the public organization is expected to play a more substantial role, e.g. by contributing time, money or even a political decision. That's where things can sometimes go wrong. It may sometimes seem like a social issue is not being addressed, when behind the scenes the government is working on procedures, negotiations or a cohesive vision. In such cases, the government is working on providing context for other types of coalition.

Take the example of the brownfield site (see above): imagine the government had a lawsuit running against the party responsible for contaminating the site or that maybe there were several sites like this in the municipality for which a cohesive vision was being sought to be able to set to work. In these cases, the government is working on providing context for the directing role. Another possibility could be that the government was in negotiations with a project developer who'd wanted to build something on the site. In that case, the government was working in a partnering role to address the issue.

By initiating a bottom-up movement, a designer may disrupt the process that a public organization is working on behind the scenes and sooner or later face resistance from that very same organization. That resistance may seem unexpected given that no one appears to be dealing with the issue. The designer may have thought that the government was stuck with a problem and would be happy to at least have one party that was full of energy that wanted to tackle things.

A designer in an autonomous role will find it far more difficult to gauge what role a public organization plays or wants to play. This is an important focus area—all the more so, given that the facilitating role the designer expects the public organization to play cannot be managed in a traditional sense and as such is usually the least favourite option. The public organization will only want to take on that role if all the other options have been exhausted.

Key Ideas in This Chapter

↳ Representatives from public organizations can work with other parties in three different roles:

  ↳ A directing role: this is part of a directive coalition, where the organization's own ambition is paramount. This type of coalition is based on achieving a concrete result.

  ↳ A partnering role: this is part of a coalition where the parties draw up a shared ambition and need each other to achieve this. This type of coalition is based on achieving goals.

  ↳ A facilitating role: this is part of a connective coalition. Movement is encouraged that contributes to the unifying ambition of all stakeholders. This type of coalition is based on facilitating movement.

↳ Wicked problems in particular require public organizations to take on a facilitating role. Facilitating can be done in several ways: by giving attention to the issue, by spending time, resources or money on it, through policy or policy tools, or showing clear commitment, e.g. by a director of a public organization participating in a ribbon-cutting ceremony.

↳ A connective coalition can't be managed in a traditional manner and as such will generally be regarded by public organizations as the least popular way of working together.

↪   Designers can help with this by building connective
     coalition relationships around a wicked problem.
     For instance, by using empathic research to uncover
     the motivations of stakeholders and by framing
     the problem around these motivations, designers can
     develop a connective and inviting ambition.

↪   In a coalition between several parties, there are a
     number of processes that occur on the boundary of
     the organizations involved. The professionals working
     on that boundary must be able to switch between
     different roles when working with others. Boundary
     spanners and designers complement each other seam-
     lessly. Chapter 4 is all about the work that boundary
     spanners do in practice.

Design Thinking and Stakeholder Management

At every public organization, there are professionals who maintain contact with end–users, and together they work on finding solutions. The work they do goes beyond the boundary of the organization they represent. In this book, these professionals are referred to as 'boundary spanners'; they are the link between the end–users' life-world and the public organizations' systems. Boundary spanners experience like no one else the tension between doing things right, i.e. according to the system, and doing the right thing, i.e. for society. This chapter will show how design thinking is as much a promising addition to the repertoire of boundary spanners, as it is essential

Doing things right doesn't always mean doing the right thing.

LIFE-WORLD AND SYSTEMS WORLD

The classification into life-world and a 'world' of systems is an oft-used one. Van der Lans[25] defines these two 'worlds' as follows: "Systems are everything that people have developed into institutions and structures in fields such as economics, politics, education, science, government, healthcare, the welfare state, etc. It's an extraordinarily diverse collection of systems and subsystems. The life-world is the world of experience, in which people deal with each other in and outside the systems."

The distinction between the life-world and the systems world is often considered a problem, the key argument being that these two 'worlds' are finding it increasingly difficult to communicate with each other. Although I know of many examples that underline this, my view is that both worlds serve a function and that the issue is not so much about scrapping the differences, but about using these in a productive fashion. That's the starting point for this chapter.

WORKING ACROSS THE BOUNDARY BETWEEN TWO WORLDS

Boundary spanners are the professionals working on behalf of a public organization across the boundary between the systems of their organization and the life-world of the end-users. End-users are citizens, residents, pupils, patients, road users, etc., depending on the nature of the service being provided.

Boundary spanners represent a small group of people at public organizations. This may come as a surprise given that it's often said in the public sector that end-users should take centre stage. Yet, in practice, there's a limited group of people who actually maintain contact with the outside world. The majority of the professionals are 'inside' and, in professional terms, they have very little contact with the end-users of public services. I differentiate between two groups of boundary spanners: those with two feet grounded in the 'real world' of communities and those with one foot in a public organization and one foot outside.

In terms of the first group of boundary spanners, their work in society mainly concerns the wellbeing of individuals or groups, e.g. local police, community workers, youth workers or community nurses. These professionals are often people-oriented (and thus not system-oriented), so align well with designers. Because public organizations have grown bigger and steer things based on targets and protocols, these boundary spanners often lose the connection somewhat with their own organization. To do what's necessary, it's even wise for them to maintain a certain distance from their own organization and deviate from the protocols developed in systems. This group is surprisingly often left out of change management assignments as a key expert by their own organization. Or, as one of these boundary spanners put it: "we're the people who get energy from outside and lose it again inside." In a design process, these boundary spanners are of inestimable value to be able to reach the target group and to act as a sounding board. However, they have limited influence on the system side of the issue, e.g. the policy agenda, budget allocation and the description of their own duties. As such, to safeguard change in the organization often requires seeking out other people.

For that reason, this chapter will focus on the second type of boundary spanner, i.e. those with one foot in a public organization and another in the environment where the specific social issue is playing out. This group includes such people as stakeholder managers. Stakeholder managers are increasingly seen on large spatial planning projects and other developments that are socially sensitive, e.g. the increase in flight movements or the arrival of a refugee centre. They are the public organization's face to the outside world, but their involvement is limited both in terms of content and time horizon by the objective of a project or a programme. In both cases, their collaboration is a temporary one, aimed at achieving a unique result or a particular objective[26].

In a strategic project, the stakeholder manager ensures that stakeholders can provide input and commit themselves as much as possible to the proposals (to be developed). In this case, it's not just about the end-users, but also about all stakeholders. In implementation projects, the stakeholder manager's role is to prevent any 'upset' in the contact with the outside world, such as legal proceedings, negative press and social and political unrest. Stakeholder managers also help deliver an assignment on time and within budget.

I realize that 'stakeholder management' is an unfortunate term; it's not as if stakeholders allow themselves to be managed. As for wicked problems, that's hardly ever the case (if one at all), as outlined in chapter 3. Although terms like 'stakeholder engagement' or 'enabling stakeholder collaboration' may better reflect what is meant[27], this book sticks to the term 'stakeholder management' because it's the most widely used.

MUTUAL GAINS APPROACH

Stakeholder managers usually work in an intuitive fashion. If their work can be based on a particular methodology, then it's generally the mutual gains approach (MGA)[28]. In essence, this is a negotiating approach that seeks to benefit all parties. Taking a win-win approach to situations is in line with a public sector that takes decisions based on collective interests, with an eye for those in the minority. As such, the MGA repertoire is a big step forward compared to a standard negotiation, where the participating parties are only working towards their own interests.

In many cases, MGA offers stakeholder managers a solid foundation to help achieve the desired project or programme results. There are limitations to MGA however, and that's exactly where design thinking comes in handy.

HOW DO YOU ENGAGE STAKEHOLDERS?

Stakeholder managers work inside a public organization as part of a bigger project or programme team. They often combine a cognitive style of change management (in the form of project-based work) and a negotiating style of change management. After all, these are the predominant styles of change management at public organizations.

In practice, their way of working looks like this: a boundary is drawn around an issue and inside that boundary all the stakeholders are uniformly invited to participate in a project, e.g. either by letter or through a website. Meetings are organized at a location accessible to everyone at a time convenient to most.

That's an efficient way of working, and in terms of the system it makes sense too: all the stakeholders get access to the process in the same manner, thereby safeguarding equality before the law. Nevertheless, this seemingly objective and honest approach leaves many key stakeholders out of the process. Some end-users are literally not seen. Others don't feel invited because for them the communication is written in an incomprehensible language and in inaccessible forms, i.e. in letters or on a website.

A large municipality was about to start discussions with the neighbourhood about planned restructuring. However, the project leader was not at all convinced that the municipality's story would be in line with the residents' experience.

The neighbourhood in question had already experienced a participation project a few years ago that had not gone as planned, so I was asked to take another look at what was going on in the neighbourhood with one of the members of my team.

We spoke to a lot of people. Those that were able to tell us the most about what was going on in the neighbourhood were the hotdog sellers (see figure 12). They've had a spot in the area for more than a decade, they know everyone well and see what happens to the others: "This street is our television." And yet, they'd never been invited by the municipality to collaborate on the intended restructuring. On enquiry, we learned why: they didn't have an address in the neighbourhood and as such didn't receive any letters inviting them to the residents evening.

Fig. 12: Not everyone who has great knowledge of a local situation is a resident.

94

If particular stakeholders are not reached, then the stakeholder manager leaves valuable knowledge unused. As such, it pays to go looking for stakeholders in a different way. Fieldwork is the most obvious option. In the case studies in this chapter, the public organizations were open to fieldwork. But this approach has often led to resistance, with reactions like: "Two afternoons outside, looking around? I don't have time for that!" and "Everyone got a letter. Our responsibility has to stop somewhere." I've often been surprised that residents meetings are deemed to have been successful when the majority of the community hasn't even been reached.

CASE STUDY PART 1

THE A9 LAND TUNNEL

Part of the A9 project was building a land tunnel more than three kilometres long in a densely populated and multicultural area. The stakeholder managers were fairly easily able to gauge who the stakeholders would be, e.g. nearby residents who'd experience noise pollution from the pile-driving, people who'd be affected by traffic disruptions and the (parents of the) children who'd face heavy duty vehicles on their journey to and from school. These were the real issues that stakeholder managers wanted to deal with carefully, and rightfully so (see figures 13 and 14).

As such, the invitation to a residents meeting highlighted these interests. Oddly enough, only a part of the community came to the meeting. The project team may have had a full room in the first few meetings, but

this room was in no way representative of the neighbourhood. Various ethnicities live in the area and the population, on average, is very young. But the room only contained white, higher-educated people, (way) over forty years of age. Were the other groups not concerned about the disruptions? Not worried about the safety of the children? This didn't seem likely to the stakeholder managers. My team worked with them to find other ways to reach the neighbourhood and bring people together.

We had to find the people who were not in that room, and there was nothing else to do other than to go out and find them in the neighbourhood. We were supported in this by a number of boundary spanners from the municipality: community workers, street coaches and staff from

Fig. 13: Impression of the A9 construction site.

economic affairs. They introduced us to the key social, economic and cultural players and helped us to discover Amsterdam Zuidoost.

We started to see that the standard communication tools on the A9 project wouldn't have any effect on them. Many people in the neighbourhood aren't fluent in Dutch, get stressed by letters from official bodies or simply have something more pressing on their minds. The municipality had learned that what works well was keeping contact with leaders in the community and using other channels, like the churches and the thirty (!) radio stations in the area.

WHAT INTERESTS AND INTRINSIC MOTIVATIONS ARE AT PLAY?

An important starting point for MGA is that you can achieve a win-win situation if you negotiate with each other on the basis of interests and not on the basis of standpoints. After all, standpoints are changeable, while interests are more or less consistent. As such, a stakeholder manager is always focussed on interests that could be damaged, e.g. deterioration in quality of life, issues that could affect (social) safety, etc. To ensure these interests do not lead to resistance that can delay a project or programme, stakeholders are invited to learn about the project or programme and given the opportunity to participate in them and even collaborate.

This is the negotiating side of a stakeholder manager's approach. They try to find a common ground in the players' interests and reach consensus through a negotiating process. This, too, sounds very public-oriented. However, in practice, people often have very different concerns and motivations than those predicted by the public organization. As a result, no broad or deep understanding is achieved. In the case of design thinking, these concerns and motivations are revealed through empathic research[29], something that section 6.2 addresses in more detail.

Fig. 14: Impression of the A9 construction site.

DESIGN THINKING AND STAKEHOLDER MANAGEMENT

THE A9 LAND TUNNEL

Based on their knowledge of the project, the project organization had come up with a list of the interests in the area that could be at risk. In practice, however, these interests weren't the biggest concern in the area. This became clear when collaborating with the designers. The designers didn't use their fieldwork to find out how the residents wanted to relate to the tunnel; instead they were far more interested in the residents' deepest daily concerns and motivations.

The fieldwork helped paint a picture of what was going on in the neighbourhood, and that had very little to do with mobility and accessibility or the impact of a large building project. We saw a neighbourhood where many people were dealing with poverty, school drop-outs and unemployment, but also a neighbourhood with strong social structures, entrepreneurship and pride in the area. We heard some poignant stories that left an impression.

Slowly, but surely, we realized that 'talent development' was the central theme in this neighbourhood. So many initiatives — both bottom-up and from the government — had been set up to help young people get basic qualifications, on to the job market and to make smart financial decisions — all fundamental things to be able to progress in life. This also explained the turnout in the room: if you're busy trying to get a handle on your future, then the likelihood of you going to hear about a land tunnel being built is nil.

The research led to a much clearer conclusion: if the project team wanted to build ties with a broad cross-section of the community, it would make little sense to seduce the area into relating to the project. The project would instead have to relate to the residents' everyday lives. In which case, a project on talent development had to be developed alongside one about the building disruption.

How is it possible that residents meetings are deemed to have been successful when the majority of the community hasn't even been reached?

THREE COALITION ROLES FOR
THE STAKEHOLDER MANAGER

Chapter 3 outlined the three roles that a public organization can play in a coalition with end-users: a directing role, a partnering role and a facilitating role.

Stakeholder management switches between using a directing role and partnering role. Public organizations have a clear objective and direct the process. They decide who'll be involved, when this will happen and what it will be about, as well as how intense the participation will be, i.e. informing, advising or collaborating on decisions. This is all part of the directing role.

MGA does something quite unique however. First of all, by distributing the right information, it equips people to take a seat at the table as a fully-fledged discussion partner with public organizations and to promote their own interests. And it doesn't stop there. MGA often uses the expression "to enlarge the pie"[30], which means increasing the playing field for negotiation by creating new values. As result, there's more to share. Also, this turns the public organization's coalition role into one of a partnering role.

Enlarging the pie might fail, however, if the stakeholders aren't interested in the newly created values. If that's the case, then there's not much reason to enlarge the pie and something entirely different has to be put on the table instead.

In design terms, we don't talk in 'pies', but in 'frames'. A frame is a way of looking at things. And by reframing an issue, the perspective from which you look at the issue changes. Also, reframing an issue can create an entirely new collaborative reality. After reframing an issue, people who at first didn't feel welcome to develop a relationship with a project see opportunities to build a connection based on their own motivations. This makes a project less of a threat and more of an opportunity. Instead of it being a negotiation process, it becomes a co-creative one. This co-creative process requires public organizations to take on a different coalition role, namely a facilitating one. Design thinking in this case is as much a promising addition to the negotiating repertoire of stakeholder managers, as it is essential.

The deeply personal contact that design thinking assumes is not expected of stakeholder managers. MGA even encourages a professional distance: "separate the people from the problem, place the detailed problem centre stage and don't make it personal."[31] I understand this approach. Stakeholder managers don't always have it easy; they're often spoken to about an organization's plans—and not in a polite way either. For instance, the owner of a fast-food joint let one of the stakeholder managers in the central case study in this chapter know that he wouldn't hesitate to "deep-fry parts of the stakeholder manager" if the project was given the go-ahead. Keeping a professional distance helps stakeholder managers to continue to work in a project-oriented fashion, but it's difficult to combine this with the empathic approach required when an assignment concerns a wicked problem.

CASE STUDY PART 3

THE A9 LAND TUNNEL

A meeting about limiting disruption was not interesting enough to the people in the neighbourhood for them to get actively involved in the A9 project team. So how could the neighbourhood be inspired to get involved?

Thanks to our fieldwork, we knew that talent development was the most important theme in the neighbourhood. How could the A9 project address that? The designers realized that building the land tunnel would mean a lot of people, machines and technology coming into the area and that a lot of goods and services would have to be bought in. This got my team thinking of a temporary economy. But a temporary economy will get off to a bad start if you build a physical and mental fence around it.

As such, my team suggested to approach the project like a temporary economy and to set up a social enterprise that would support intrinsically motivated neighbourhood residents in their talent development. The frame (building site = disruption) didn't help us get the majority of residents to the table, but once we decided to reframe the project (building site = temporary economy), we were able to develop a wide social interest.

We called the social enterprise Buurbouw, which is a combination of the Dutch words 'buur' (neighbour) and 'bouw' (build) that evokes the trustworthy image of a 'buurvrouw' (a female neighbour). We also created a logo and a website[32]. The stakeholder managers from the ministry and the contractor, and boundary spanners from the municipality promoted the Buurbouw at every opportunity. But what was even more important was that a different tone had been set in the day-to-day contact with the neighbourhood. The disruption, which certainly existed, wasn't hidden away. But there was a constant consideration for the other side of the project too, i.e. the unique opportunity to learn or develop something because of the A9 project.

WAAR DE A9 EN AMSTERDAM ZUID-OOST ELKAAR ONTMOETEN.

SYNERGY BETWEEN DESIGN THINKING AND STAKEHOLDER MANAGEMENT

As a field of expertise, stakeholder management has developed a lot in the past few years, with MGA ideas providing a methodological foundation. But there are two aspects of stakeholder management that MGA doesn't address, for which design thinking can offer an additional repertoire.

First and foremost, the MGA repertoire works on win-win situations. This suggests that there's a liberating idea behind stakeholder management. After all, most stakeholders have to get to grips with becoming a fully-fledged conversation partner of public organizations. And this is where the biggest issue with MGA arises: that liberating idea is not genuinely fleshed out for enough people. In practice, MGA is mainly relevant to the people who are able to promote their

Public sector
innovators
dare to sail
by their own
moral compass.

interests and know how to get to speak to different organizations. For a large part of the population, the processes of public organizations remain inaccessible, difficult to understand and untrustworthy.

The second aspect is that, in essence, MGA has a repertoire for negotiation, which doesn't suit wicked issues that require a co-creative approach. Stakeholder managers may want to defer to co-creative processes more often, but in many cases they lack the repertoire for that. MGA doesn't provide for that either. Design thinking can help public organizations with this, e.g. by identifying the unusual suspects, employing forms of communication and communication channels that suit the target group, engaging people based on their intrinsic motivation and not on the basis of interests and standpoints, and developing a shared, inviting frame. Chapter 6 will cover all of this in detail.

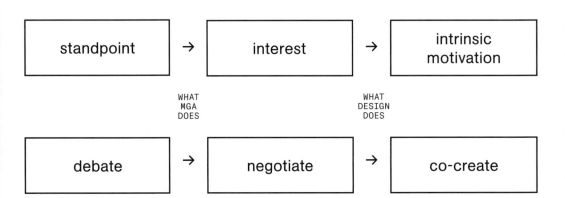

WHAT MGA DOES

WHAT DESIGN DOES

Fig. 15: The processes that MGA and design enable.

Because stakeholder managers work beyond the boundaries of their own organization, they're often the first ones to recognize when the additional repertoire of design thinking would be preferable. They can also play an important role in aligning the life-world and the systems. What I mean by that is that the decision to take a design approach can lead to friendly fire because the public organization experiences it as an approach that puts pressure on the organization's core values, as explained in chapters 2 and 3.

Fig. 16: Children in Amsterdam Zuidoost participating in Buurbouw.

THE A9 LAND TUNNEL

The Buurbouw helped establish a co-creative process, as opposed to a negotiating one. That process required that public organizations take on a different role, namely a facilitating one — a role that the stakeholder managers eagerly carried out. They knew how to speak to residents about their entrepreneurship and connection with the area. This led to a large number of impressive results, such as the following.

A large amount of the wood from the trees that were cut down went to Stadshout Amsterdam[33]. This organization creates meeting places for the city and communities. Neighbourhood projects were developed and brought to life by designers, craftsmen (in training) and residents. Playground equipment and street furniture was made as part of the project; this ended up in the park on the roof of the tunnel. A bench for Mrs. Van Teeffelen was made, too. Her now deceased husband had (illegally) planted a cypress tree once upon a time and this tree now had to be cut down. Wood from this tree was used to make the bench that now sits in her garden.

There were a lot of complaints from the neighbourhood when the piles for the foundations were being noisily driven into the ground. This work continued throughout the spring, including the time before the exam period. Because of the noise, the children found it difficult to concentrate. The Buurbouw provided a quiet study area and asked two local tutoring institutes to take on the supervision. All 150 children passed: the highest pass rate ever. And not despite the project, but thanks to it.

One of the residents, Dave, also endured the daily racket. The stakeholder managers discovered that he actually wanted to be a caterer, specifically to make sandwiches. But because of all the stress, he didn't get his business going. It was agreed that the Buurbouw would be his first customer. What started of as a one-time thing turned into a permanent relationship with all the Buurbouw parties, i.e. the contractor, the state and the municipality. What's more, during the A9 project, Dave also got other customers, which means that his business will continue once the project is finished[34].

There was also a lot of knowledge-sharing with the schools in the area in particular. Those building the A9 gave engineering lessons, but also showed that large machines have potentially dangerous blind spots. Also, under the supervision of a biologist, children helped plant the verges and protect fauna, like bats and birds (see figure 16).

One of the stakeholder managers spotted a man with a camera rummaging around the building site a few times. He proved to be an enthusiastic amateur photographer.

Ordinarily, someone like that would've been sent away to prevent any accidents in and around the building site. In this case, however, he was given a vest, a hardhat and a pair of boots, and the telephone number of the site foreman. The photos he took were used on the building site fences and on the project website. The man even organized photography workshops on the building site for young people in the neighbourhood.

A stakeholder manager can respond to this together with the designer. Stakeholder managers know like no one else where the boundaries for an acceptable solution lie.

Stakeholder managers who emerge as innovators in public organizations know how things work at their organizations and what's needed to stretch the boundaries of what's possible.

STAKEHOLDER MANAGEMENT AND FRIENDLY FIRE

Design thinking can help to reframe a wicked problem and to establish a co-creative coalition with the community. However, there are some things about design thinking that, although well intended, could lead to friendly fire, obstruction or even sabotage of the design process by the public organizations involved.

The beginning of this chapter talked about the reactions you could get as a stakeholder manager taking a broad approach to the field: "no one has any time for that!" and "our responsibility has to end somewhere". Being goal-oriented and efficient sometimes impedes an empathic approach. Secondly, permitting experience can prompt a systemic response. For instance, if parents complain that their kids can't concentrate because of the noise, a systemic response would be to first establish whether that noise does indeed breach the (system) norms and then investigate what the generic measures would be in cases like this. It's clear that this doesn't help the children at all. Proposing generic solutions is done based on the predominant core values of being efficient and goal-oriented. But equality before the law and functionality (i.e. socially responsible costs) also pose limitations on getting too involved with people. After all, the more specifically a stakeholder experiences a problem, the more specific the solution will be. The systemic resistance integral to this will be expressed as "you're creating a precedent."

A third form of friendly fire comes from reframing. The project organization expects the stakeholder manager to be working on preventing resistance in the community. If the stakeholder manager reframes an issue to come up with meaningful solutions together with stakeholders, this may provoke systemic resistance: "that's not part of our job!" The suggestion that the stakeholder manager is just playing around a bit is not far off in that case.

CASE STUDY PART 5

THE A9 LAND TUNNEL

Two years after my team delivered the concept of the Buurbouw, I looked back on the project with the project leader in question and one of the stakeholder managers[35]. How was friendly fire avoided in this project? In this case, this was achieved because of a combination of factors.

Firstly, the role of the stakeholder managers and the project manager involved was crucial. They weren't happy with the fact that a large number of the residents hadn't been reached. They dared to sail by their own moral compass.

A second success factor was because the initiatives they facilitated were very easy to explain to the community and didn't require any complicated decision-making. "For pragmatic solutions, you don't always have to consult the entire organization first.

There'll always be people to explain to you why something can't be done. And before you know it, you're too late and you can't do anything meaningful anymore. The thing is to simply set to work and defend your actions." Once done, few people could criticize the action. "Even small initiatives were seen by the community, and in practice this never once led to the dreaded precedent effect."

The third success factor was the fact that there was a need to do things differently. The project team realized that a big project in a built-up area would have a big impact and that standard stakeholder management wouldn't suffice. In this case, the construction of a new underground line in Amsterdam loomed large over the project organization. This building project had seen some huge delays and overshot its budget more than once, in part because communities turned against the building process. The need to do things differently was also because the municipality had made an official request for jobs to be created as part of the A9 project for residents with poor employment opportunities. In practice, this type of request can cause a lot of upset. If it's not followed through properly, the municipality can increase the pressure by delaying the process for issuing permits — something that we'd already seen in the case study for the Best Detour of the Netherlands. Deterrents and external threats are often a perfect argument to do things differently for once.

The final success factor was because the Buurbouw led to a pleasant form of contact with the community that satisfied all parties involved. Usually, the interaction between a project and the community is a lot of back and forth about noise and disruption, with a sigh of relief and a sense of pride at the end of the journey when the work is done. In this case, there were compliments being given during the construction phrase. For instance, a resident even said on the radio: "we've found a friend in the ministry."[36]

Key Ideas in
This Chapter

↳ Boundary spanners are public sector staff who maintain contact with the community. On a day-to-day basis, they are the natural party for designers to work with.

↳ Boundary spanners with two feet in the community are often indispensable in a design-thinking process. They can offer access to end-users and act as a valuable sounding board for the designers. However, as they operate far outside the organization, they often can't help to guarantee changes at an organizational or system level.

↳ Boundary spanners with one foot in their public organization and one outside do potentially have the power to change things. One example of this type of boundary spanner is the stakeholder manager.

↳ As a field of expertise, stakeholder management has become far more professional in the past few years, with the mutual gains approach (MGA) offering a methodological foundation. MGA is a step forward, but also has limitations that design thinking can answer.

↳ MGA is focused on a negotiating process based on people's interests. Design thinking, on the other hand, is a co-creative process based on intrinsic motivations. As such, design thinking is a welcome and essential addition to the MGA repertoire.

↳   A public organization may find starting with design thinking appealing in particular cases, such as when there's an external pressure, when negotiating doesn't provide an answer or when a genuinely liberating ambition provides the foundation for stakeholder management.

Chapter 5

Design Thinking and Power

The previous chapters showed that wicked problems can be dealt with effectively in a co-creative coalition, with space for stakeholders' intrinsic motivations. Design thinking is of added value here. That being said, co-creative coalitions are difficult to force on the sources of power that public organizations are familiar with, thereby creating a need for different sources of power. This chapter covers the sources of power that designers draw on and also discusses how the right synergy can be found with the traditional sources of power of a public organization.[37]

Designers
may not hold
a position of
power, but they
can exercise
power.

POWER—AN OVERVIEW

Power is the ability to influence. People have power if they can influence someone else's convictions, attitude and/or behaviour[38]. What is and isn't allowed? Are we going left or right? How will resources be shared? But also: who's allowed to participate and who's on the sidelines? And what are the rules of the game of working together?

Power is linked to hierarchy. It's evident to everyone that a CEO or alderman has power; these are positions of power. This 'positional power' is not the only source of power however. Designers don't hold a position of power, yet they can exercise power. They have other sources of power that this chapter refers to as 'personal power'.

POSITIONAL POWER

Positional power is linked to hierarchy and as such to a certain extent easy to understand in the public sector. It's public knowledge how power structures are organized, who has a political role and what their profile and mandate is. Political ambitions are outlined in public documents too, including the investment agenda to be able to achieve these ambitions. Anyone who wants to can figure out how positional power is organized in the public sector.

For designers, having a certain political insight is essential. You have to know where responsibilities and authorities lie to be able to give positional power a place in the design process. After all, a proposal can generally only be executed if a decision has been made, e.g. about money or other resources, or when there's political support. That's why a designer at least needs to know who makes those decisions. Political knowledge is also useful to be able to know how to keep a design process under the radar, so that a proposal has the space to grow. But you also need to know how to showcase a design process, so that you can increase the movement around it.

Although public sector staff are very familiar with positional power, this is often not the case outside these organizations—and designers are no exception. In my view, this is partly due to the fact that design courses don't spend a lot of time on the governance side of social issues. As such, what's unknown remains unloved. What's more, many people—and not just designers—have negative connotations with positional power. Positional power is often associated with a lack of transparency (i.e. backroom deals), cronyism and untrustworthiness, or with processes that are only focussed on keeping or increasing power. When incidents occur, they're generally widely discussed. It's no surprise then that many people would rather keep out of the way when it comes to positional power.

Although this shadowy side of positional power is undeniable, it's also a bit of a caricature. Even in a healthy democracy, acquiring and maintaining positional powerful is an inseparable part of the decision-making processes. By accepting that, it's also easier to see that positional power "(…) is not a problem to be solved, but a mystery that wants to be discovered."[39]

DEBATE PART 1

DESIGN THINKING IN GOVERNMENT

During Dutch Design Week[40] I organized a debate between three public administrators about the use of design thinking in government: Mary-Ann Schreurs, alderwomen of the municipality of Eindhoven, Anne-Marie Spierings, vice-governor of the province of Noord-Brabant, and Peter Glas chairman of the De Dommel water board.

I'd invited these public administrators because all three are important ambassadors of design thinking in government. Moreover, Eindhoven is home to Dutch Design Week and the Design Academy. The debate was mainly attended by designers and civil servants who actively participated in the discussion. As an introduction, I asked the room — to be

118

sure — whether everyone was familiar with what the positions of alderwomen, vice-governor and chairman of the water board entailed. What I'd suspected proved to be true: most of the designers conceded they didn't know. I asked the tutors attending from the various courses whether they offered their students public administration as a subject, and they said no.

The public administrators attending were surprisingly restrained in their response. I suspect they'd noticed this before and accepted it. I say 'surprisingly' because public sector staff and consultants are expected to be sensitive to the complexities of (politics and) governance. The general response, also from the civil servants in the room who'd worked with designers, was: "we get the designer up to speed."

Although I believe a basic knowledge of public administration is necessary for designers to be successful in a coalition with public organizations, the outstretched hand of these public organizations will also be essential as long as designers are not a permanent part of the organizations.

Firstly, a delegated position of power is a constant in the real world. An administrator, e.g. an alderman, has final responsibility for the creation and implementation of policy, but there are others who work on policy on a daily basis and take responsibility for it, e.g. project directors, department heads or civil servants. A delegated position of power is not recorded in the same accessible manner. More often that not, there are no public organizational charts. Detailed plans and budgets are not easily available to everyone. As such, it's not entirely clear who you have to go to for a given issue.

Moreover, a delegated position of power is far more fluid than a public administrator's position. Project leaders can be replaced from one day to the next, while that's far less likely to happen with public administrators. For processes to run smoothly, it's important that designers be shown the ropes of a public organization at the start of a coalition between designers and public sector staff, and that designers also show an interest in this.

The second reason designers need some help to find their way at a public organization is because there's a second key source of power, namely, personal power. And that's something you're only going to experience after you've walked around an organization a bit.

PERSONAL POWER

Personal power is conferred based on who you are and not on the role you fulfil. To understand where the actual power in a position lies and how this power is exercised, personal power is just as important a positional power.

Personal power can reside in knowledge (of cases), experience, image, access to networks or information, and charisma. Look at someone you admire (or dread) professionally and ask yourself why; it's probably not because they're the boss. There are other factors that play a role. It's not just inspiring people who have personal power; people who manage to make a work environment permanently unsafe can have personal power. In both cases, people have a tendency to go the extra mile, either because of inspiration or in the hope of not being put through the wringer again.

Personal power is not organized in any formal fashion and it sometimes takes a well-trained eye to spot it. Moreover, it requires a subdued approach because unlike positional power, which you can quite easily ask people about, personal power is a far more difficult topic of conversation. Suggesting that someone has more knowledge, experience or charisma, that this person is first among equals, can be a sensitive matter. Exercising personal power can also be seen as something negative.

In a coalition between designers and public organizations, it may be clear that the position of power resides with the public organization. But wicked problems require an ability to connect people to a given issue and find a solution for it together. In that case, positional power is not enough and personal power is indispensible. Many people can have this personal power, designers included. The next section discusses five sources of power that designers (can) use[41].

A DESIGNER'S POWER: INSPIRATION

One of the more obvious sources of a designer's power is the inspiration they can bring to the table, i.e. not saying how things should be done, but showing people how things can be done (differently) and making things conceivable. Or in the words of a 22-year-old undergraduate designer speaking to a group of experienced civil servants: "if we can think of it, then it can be created"[42].

Inspiration is a source of power that fuels enthusiasm and inspires people to want to work with you, to do things they actually don't dare to do or can't quite fully imagine. What's more, inspiration as a source of power is very mediagenic, giving designers a higher than average opportunity to showcase their story. This helps open the doors that stay closed to others.

POWER THROUGH INSPIRATION

One of the Netherlands' biggest public organizations asked Twynstra Gudde to help them to take their stakeholder management to the next level. Our proposal of course included a module on design thinking.

Manon van Hoeckel, the designer I'd enlisted for this module, told me in passing a while later that she'd had a meeting that week with the most senior director of the organization in question. He'd seen her on TV in a talent show for youngsters and been inspired by her, so wanted to know how her way of working could help his organization.

A design
process
requires
new public
leadership.

My colleagues were very surprised when they discovered that of the members of their team, comprising senior consultants and a single designer, it was the designer who was closest to the organization's biggest boss. And this designer was the youngest member of the team by far as well.

A DESIGNER'S POWER: EMPATHY

Everyone who's part of the problem should be able to be part of the solution—that sounds like something that few people would object to, right? This, however, requires that you understand what motivates people at a very deep level. Designers start with people, without the interference of the system. As such, little stands in the way of the designers and the end-users. As people, designers are no more empathetic than others per se, but they are better equipped at using that empathetic ability in a professional setting thanks to their mentality, methods and tools.

This source of power helps them to quickly figure out what the social fabric of a situation is. This helps to be able to maintain an easy and relaxed form of contact with end-users—something that many public organizations are really crying out for.

POWER THROUGH EMPATHY

As part of the process of writing this book, I visited leading theatre director Adelheid Roosen[43], whose work typically forges a great intimacy and sense of connection between people.

Her work includes a series of neighbourhood safaris called WijkSafari's. These were each set in a different neighbourhood in different cities (including Amsterdam Zuidoost from the case study in chapter 4) and they tell the story of the neighbourhood in question using the lives of the residents as a foundation (see figure 17).

The WijkSafari's leave a big

impression on the audience because the actors bring to life what motivates the residents and what holds them back, e.g. what it means to grow up and live in a particular neighbourhood. To really get to know the heart and soul of the neighbourhood and the residents, the actors spend a few weeks as houseguests of the neighbourhood residents. "I'm often asked how I find the residents, but that comes naturally thanks to the form of research we use. Knocking on doors, sitting back and listening on house visits, and going anywhere and everywhere. I don't have any protocols for that and simply follow my intuition. If the story moves me and the resident wants to take part, then their story will be in the performance. I don't hold any kind of audition or test."

When speaking to Adelheid, she summed up the essence of empathic research nicely: "To understand someone else, I have to touch the other person, and that can only happen if I want to be touched myself. I learned to play rage by examining by own rage. I had to learn where my shyness was, where my crying resides." This is quite possibly the biggest task of empathic research: allowing someone's loneliness to also be about your loneliness. That radicalization of youth is also about your radicalization. Adelheid quotes the philosopher Emmanuel Levinas: "I become myself in the face of the other."

I, too, believe that she and people like her can inspire the public sector with their knowledge and experience. "Apart from education in art and design, there's no place at all in teaching for experimenting, doing things wrong, stumbling, failure, crying, literally undressing. You can't believably step onto a stage if you do so at a distance, if you do so using the same detached language of civil servants. If you step onto the stage like that, every acting teacher will say: "Go back and do it again." The audience wouldn't accept it either."

A DESIGNER'S POWER: PUTTING SYSTEMS TEMPORARILY ON HOLD

To really be able to place end-users and the wicked problem centre stage, you often need to put systems temporarily on

hold. Otherwise, political discussions and ideological stand-points can impede the process. And the same goes for the limitations of written and unwritten rules. But how do you do this?

Designers have various methods for that. Some simply deny systems, which incidentally isn't generally the best strategy in the long term (see the last section of this chapter). Others recognize that systems exist and make slight interventions to create the designing space. A positive side effect of this is that most, but not all, professionals in the public sector find these sorts of interventions liberating; they're also energizing.

POWER BY PUTTING SYSTEMS ON HOLD

Designers use different techniques to put systems temporarily on hold. For instance, in his co-creative work sessions Professor Kees Dorst draws a hippo up on a whiteboard, the hippo illustrating the acronym HIPPO, i.e. the highest paid person's opinion (see figure 18). "The moment that hierarchy stands in the way of the design process, I subtly refer to the HIPPO to get everyone focused again. "Ideological differences, procedures, rules and the HIPPO are no longer the most important thing for a while."

Fig. 18: The HIPPO, i.e. the highest paid person's opinion.

Lino Hellings developed PAPA, the Participating Artists' Press Agency[44]. Here, empathic research is paramount and entails a group of people going onto the streets "to decide what catches their eye" (see figure 18). The photos this activity produces are posted on the PAPA platform for a week, along with a title and short text, and at the end of the week the group distils the most important themes from these photos, etc. In this case, the pictures taken by the intern are just as important as those taken by the director. Hellings: "I wouldn't know how to do it any differently because how else would you apply a hierarchy to personal meaning?

There has to be space in the design process for ambiguity, embracing paradoxes, a holistic view, multiple standpoints. Only then will a space be created for a new shared view."

A DESIGNER'S POWER: CREATING INVITING WAYS OF WORKING

Public organizations generally operate using fixed ways of working, e.g. information evenings, sounding boards, etc., with end-users being seduced (or forced) to accept a way of working that's not very inviting to them, but which public organizations are familiar with. Because of this, there's often a certain, not unwarranted, cynicism that "things have already been decided." It's challenging to get a co-creative process off the ground as part of these ways of working.

New ways of working are required that really invite people to co-create: ways of working that people want and can relate to. What helps to create a curiosity is to give these new ways of working a look and feel that's not immediately associated with the public organization in question. If this way of working also challenges those involved on their expertise, e.g. their knowledge of the neighbourhood, they'll quickly get the feeling their contribution is essential.

I've noticed that my clients are often surprised at how quickly designers get access to groups of people that are difficult for

my clients to reach. Of course, this is partly due to designers' empathetic talents (as outlined above), but it's also due to their ability to find inviting ways of working that provide the platform for the coalition.

POWER THROUGH CREATING CHALLENGING ENTITIES

Designer Tabo Goudswaard knows like no one else that developing a fully-fledged coalition between a public organization and end-users is a question of design. He develops new entities each time that challenge and invite people to contribute. In the projects we worked on together, we created a number of new entities, like a cooperation for retiring farmers, the Buurbouw (see chapter 3), an association for public administrators and even an entirely new neighbourhood called MagStad, which translates in English to Maybourhood (see figure 20 and chapter 6.2). These all helped create a new reality, and discussing the social issues with each other in this new reality got us to the heart of the matter: what does the neighbourhood in question need and, in particular, how do people want to get involved?

DESIGNER'S POWER: AUTONOMY

Autonomy is an important source of power. But can there be autonomy within the scope of a project? I think so. Autonomy is the ability to sail by your own (moral) compass and in doing so build connections with people. This can also be done when working on a project and is probably best illustrated with a compliment my team was once given by a director: "Whenever I see your presentations, I'm always pleasantly surprised by the solutions you come up with. At the same time, however, I realize that I probably wouldn't have collaborated on these had you asked me for permission in advance."

This book mainly features case studies in which designers dealt with a social issue on behalf of a public organization.

But there are countless other wicked (social) problems that, for a whole host of reasons, public organizations cannot or will not prioritize. It's only when a promising movement arises that they want to get involved, sometimes even after they've resisted for a while. Designers appeal to people's imagination in these cases too. Take, for example, the Ocean Cleanup by Bojan Slat[45] that aims to clean up all the plastic in the ocean; or the Mine Kafon Drone designed by Massoud Hassani[46] that intends to clear landmines; or the Fair Phone created by Bas van Abel[47], a modular telephone made entirely of raw materials that have been extracted with the utmost respect for the workers and the environment.

In each case, these are problems that can justifiably be called 'wicked' and which designers have sunk their teeth into. They came up with surprising, innovative ideas and knew how to involve public and private parties to also turn these ideas into real working solutions. In this case, power from autonomy is intrinsically connected to power from inspiration.

PERSONAL POWER AND POSITIONAL POWER ARE BOTH ESSENTIAL

To influence wicked problems, public organizations and designers both need each other's sources of power. This book has already explained that positional power alone is not enough, but the same can also be said about personal power. Designers working on social issues realize that a good concept alone will not lead to the intended change. Policy and policy instruments have to be aligned with the new concept and this often requires a change in the behaviour and mentality of the many people involved, including those at public organizations. In short, a system change needs to happen and that requires an influence in processes that positional power can deliver. This positional power is something the designers do not have.

A synergy between personal and positional power can create an enormous combined power as a result, but there are three things to bear in mind.

1. A DESIGN PROCESS
   REQUIRES NEW PUBLIC
   LEADERSHIP

With social issues, it generally takes some time for a (system) change to be affected. Democracy and its periodic elections, however, mean that positional power is limited in time. A changing of the guard can have major consequences for the design process. A new public administrator who unscrupulously terminates the processes and schemes of their predecessor because of ideological differences, for instance, or the 'not invented by me' syndrome, can really damage the relationship with end-users. A design process benefits from a continuity in public administration. That means that public administrators sometimes have to go along with a movement that has been set in motion by others.

DEBATE PART 2

DESIGN THINKING IN GOVERNMENT

In the debates during Dutch Design Week, the three public administrators explained how they recognize the sources of power of designers and public organizations alike. By finding a way through that, they demonstrate the leadership required for design processes. I noted the following striking quotes from the discussions:

Mary-Ann Schreurs, alderwomen in Eindhoven: "A good design process involves communities in such a way that the public administrator can no longer ignore them. After all, as a public administrator, you can't stop a promising process that's supported by communities just because it's not to your liking."

Anne-Marie Spierings, vice-governor of the province of Noord-Brabant: "An important decision can't be taken just before a sitting public administrator is about to leave office. And a new public administrator needs some time to settle in — don't ask them questions about it then."

Peter Glas, chairman of De Dommel water board: "Both civil servants and end-users can ensure continuity. Also, if a public administrator understands a design process properly, they will not try to "cut all the ribbons" quickly just before the end of their time in office. You have to dare to let your successor bask in the success. That helps enormously to let this person demonstrate ownership."

Even if the new public administrator has an entirely different ideology than their predecessor, that doesn't have to mean the end of a design process.

Mary-Ann Schreurs: "Nobody has to change their opinion beforehand to be able to participate in a co-creative process. If it's well documented how the process will lead to a proposal, then it will be easier to assess the process and not steer things based on a given outcome. All the more so, given that the result of co-creation is to do things together and not to have the same opinion."

If the results of a design process do not lead to the required decision-making or support, this process will ultimately do more harm than good, especially if there's no motivation for it. This will lead to a (further) erosion of the relationship between end-users and the public organization. At the same time, a public administrator can commit themselves to the design process at the start of the process, but can't give carte blanche for the outcome. It's important for public administrators to understand what sources of power designers can bring to the table and how these can supplement the sources of power that public organizations have. And vice versa, of course. The ability to recognize the limits of one's own sources of power and to share power is what we call leadership.

2. WITH POWER COMES RESPONSIBILITY

"If someone exercises power over you, you may become a victim. If you're exercising power, you may abuse it. People prefer not to be a victim or a perpetrator, which is why we all act the innocent"[48].

As part of their projects, designers have a lot of power. They introduce new sources of power and create their own universe. These sources of power also bring responsibility and

Leadership is
the ability
to recognize
the limits
of your own
power and the
ability to share
that power.

some designers find that difficult to take on. The same is true for me. For instance, when people become part of a design process because I invited them, I feel a certain responsibility for them. It's not uncommon that people don't have enough time or energy or are sceptical about whether a design process will lead anywhere. Together with my team, we build up the trust between public organizations and end-users. We do that by committing ourselves to the process in a very personal way.

I can only give my commitment if the public organization legitimizes us to work on it. It's happened to me more than once that a collaborative process ends, e.g. because a new public administrator didn't prioritize the issue, and I couldn't control this. This bothers me because I can't explain to the end-users with whom I've built up a trust why the issue is no longer a priority and their involvement is also no longer required.

Although I can't control the public administrator's decision, I can control safeguarding that the design process with end-users is sufficiently anchored in the system. In other words, if after delivering our ideas they actually prove unfeasible for financial, scheduling or political reasons, then I've failed in my process leadership. I'll return to this in detail in chapter 6.

There's also another field of tension: the more experience my team and I have, the better our designs and the greater the likelihood of change. However, what's also true is that the more experience we have, the more powerful the source of power we have available to us is, and this means that the result is at risk of being more about exercising power and less about a good process. The paradox here is that the more experienced we become, the more powerful our sources of power are and the more we'll have to ask ourselves if we're using these sources of power responsibly.

3. SYSTEMS DON'T DISAPPEAR

To get the space you desperately need for a design process that places the issue and the end-users centre stage, you often have to put systems temporarily on hold. The ability to do this is a strong source of power for designers. But this ability can also come back at you like a boomerang. Positional power and systems may be put temporarily on hold, but will generally not be dismantled.

Ultimately, the outcomes of a design process continue in an arena in which positional power still plays a role, e.g. if a proposal requires a political decision (about money or policy) or political support. At the end of the day, political support, whether big or small, is a prerequisite for engagement with and the support of a public organization.

Moreover, proposals have to find a home in systems. There's a big chance that procedures, protocols and even the mentality in the system have to change for the proposal to be successful. That will only happen in practice if the people in the systems have the opportunity to become part of the process and its results, and can develop their own new perspective on how to do things. If that's not managed well enough, the proposals will become unfeasible in practice or impossible to implement. This will be addressed in the final chapter of this book.

Key Ideas in This Chapter

↳ Power is often equated with a position of power. But power is a combination of positional power and various forms of personal power.

↳ People often have negative connotations with positional power. This is understandable, but not always justified.

↳ Designers can have many different kinds of personal power in their toolbox, e.g. power from inspiration, power from empathy, power from creating inviting ways of working and power from autonomy.

↳ A successful approach to wicked problems requires a selection of sources of power—a selection that can rarely be found in just one person. A good process leader, regardless of whether they're a director, a public administrator, a stakeholder manager, a designer or something else, knows when additional sources of power are required.

↳ The ability to recognize the boundaries of your own sources of power and to share power is what we call leadership.

↳ With power, whether positional or personal, comes responsibility. Anyone who exercises their power has to do so responsibly and be prepared to take responsibility.

Chapter 6

Designing With and Within Public Organizations

The many facets of design thinking are both a valuable and essential addition to the predominant ways in which public sector issues are dealt with. That doesn't mean, however, that a proposal resulting from a carefully managed design-thinking process will automatically be successfully implemented. On the contrary, a design proposal alone generally doesn't lead to the context required for system change. This change only happens if the development of an innovative proposal is simultaneously combined with breaking down the behaviour, culture and the structures that have kept the problem alive. It also requires the development of a new perspective on how to do things that is widely supported. Chapter 6 looks at how to actively build the right context for an effective result

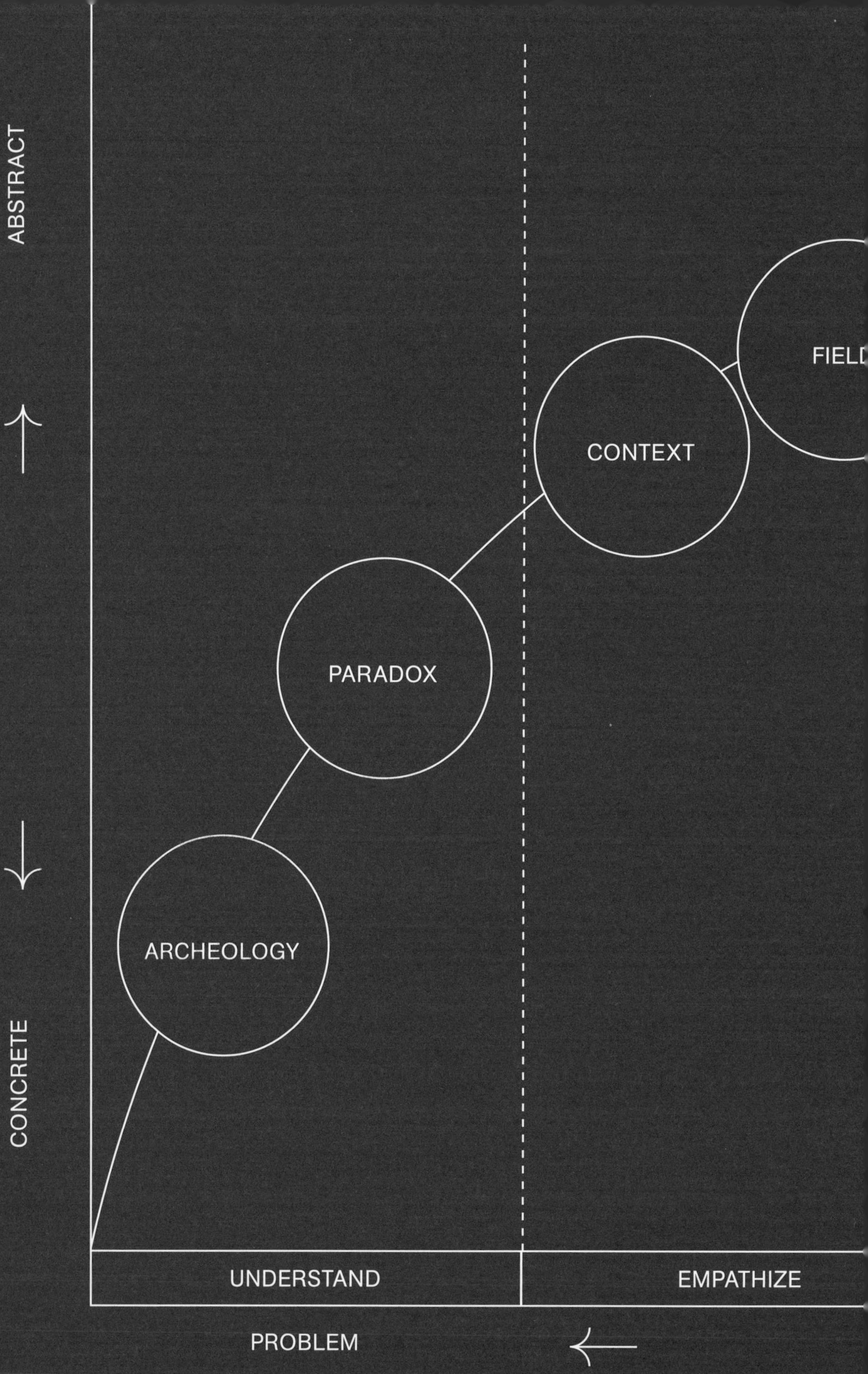
ABSTRACT
CONCRETE
FIELD
CONTEXT
PARADOX
ARCHEOLOGY
UNDERSTAND
EMPATHIZE
PROBLEM

Fig. 21: The nine steps of
frame innovation.

THEMES

FRAMES

FUTURES

TRANSFOR
MATION

INTEGRATION

CREATE NEW THINKING

TEST & ITERATE

SOLUTION

The first proposals I developed using design thinking were certainly not all implemented successfully — something that frustrated me a lot. On the one hand, that frustration stemmed from a certain vanity on my part: I wanted my work to lead to meaning-ful change. On the other hand, it was because I'd activated end-users who now felt a little abandoned and dissatisfied. I felt uncomfortable because of that: I'd increased the distance between the public organization and the end-users instead of decreasing it. And what really surprised me is that our client had seemed so happy when we wrapped up the project.

I noticed that this experience is very familiar to many designers, and I wanted to understand this. I met with my client to discuss what had hap-pened. It seemed that many in-house complica-tions arose when the results of our work were introduced. Sometimes my client couldn't clearly explain to people in the organization what the idea was behind the proposal and how we arrived at our proposals. Unfamiliarity with the design process and the design language we used also impeded the process.

Sometimes there was resistance from within the organization after we delivered a project because some (more senior) people were not involved early enough or at all, prompting a 'not invented here' reaction. Sometimes the response was simple: "that's not how we do things around here." And sometimes there was no budget or political support for the implementation.

The meeting with my clients taught me that system change doesn't just happen because there's an innovative proposal on the table. Without the repertoire to apply a new way of thinking and 'systemic support', there's a significant chance the old system will defend itself against an innovative proposal, even if there's a need for change.

The following four sections will show how a strong connection can be made between the design process and the practices of public organizations. They will cover the formulation of a research question (6.1), conducting empathic research and investigating an organization's core values (6.2), reframing (6.3) and prototyping (6.4) (see figure 21).

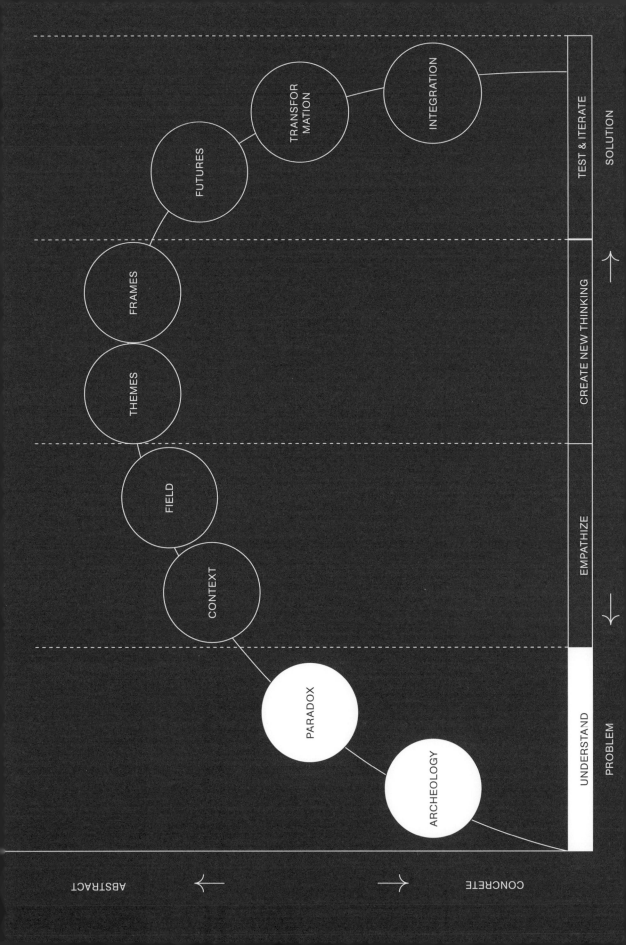

6.1 (RE)FORMULATING THE RESEARCH QUESTION

Stakeholders at a public organization are often inspired by a design approach or curious about one, but don't have a lot of experience with one yet. Although people are prepared to start something they don't quite have a full grasp of yet in terms of process, what often happens next is that they draw up an assignment or question in the way they always do. This minimizes the design space for creating meaningful proposals, which in turn leads to complications down the line. To prevent this from happening, it helps when both parties spend time together to find the right research question, as the example below illustrates.

EXAMPLE: SERVICES
FOR BENEFIT RECIPIENTS

A government authority wants to make the services for unemployment benefit recipients more efficient. On the one hand, procedures have become too complicated and resulted in clients needing additional support, while on the other hand there's an impression that the current system is being misused.

Possible formulations for the assignment:
1.   Design the services in such a way that the costs resulting from inefficiencies are reduced to a socially acceptable level.

2.   Design a new web interface that helps to reduce the costs resulting from the inefficiency of the unemployment benefit payments to 1% of the budget.

3.   Design a process that helps to increase the effectiveness of the services by aligning these with the skills, knowledge and needs of the clients.

Fig. 22: The nine steps of frame innovation – phase 'understand'.

4.   Design a number of positive corrective incentives
        in the interface with the clients that motivate them
        to provide the correct information on time.

5.   Design solutions for the obstacles clients experience
        when correctly applying for unemployment benefit.

At first glance, these all appear to be design questions, but
the scope for a design approach is very different for each
one. After all, some of the formulations are only disguised
as design issues. Behind each of the formulations lies a
predominant style of change management (see chapter 2).

The first formulation implies a negotiating process based on
what is 'socially acceptable'. This appears to suggest lots of
scope for design, as there initially seems to be no direction
given in terms of outcome. However, that can actually often
be the case in practice. If this question is asked from a law-
and-order type of perspective and dealing with misuse is the
central feature, then the proposal will be accepted. That
won't happen if the viewpoint from other proposals assumes
a more positive view of mankind. With this formulation, it's
the ideology of the person asking the question that's paramount and not the end-user.

The second formulation assumes a project-based approach,
with a clear objective and result. Here, too, the scope for
design is limited. The method that will be used to find the
solution has already been fixed, i.e. a web interface, and the
desired effect has been quantified already as well. As such,
a designer can add very little to this other than fleshing out
a preconceived solution.

The third formulation examines clients' needs in a learning
process. This offers the starting points that most designers
can use. End-users are front and centre, the method is yet
to be decided and the formulation allows for the issue
to be reframed.

Not every
question
a designer
is asked
is a design
question.

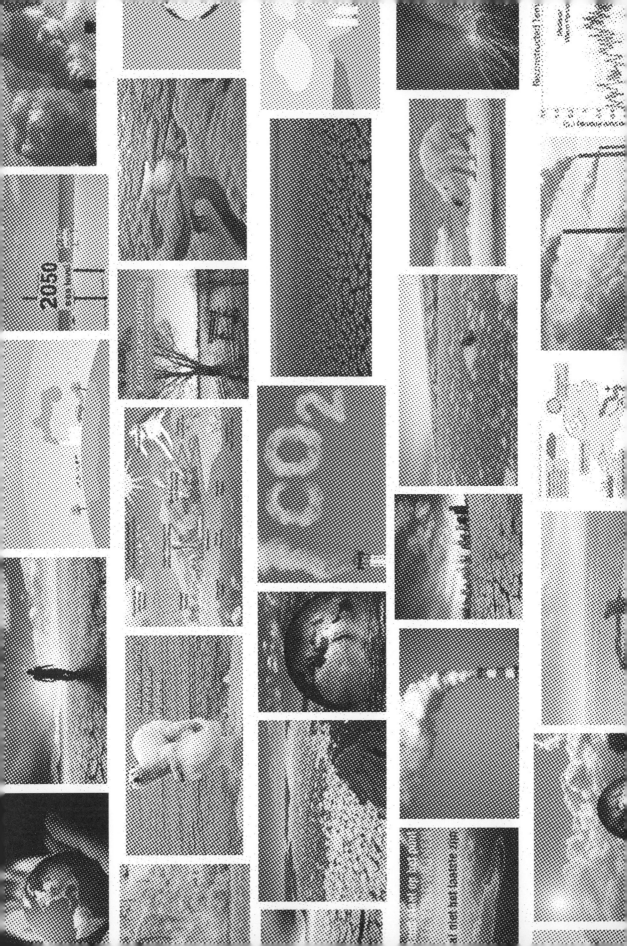

The fourth formulation is based on rewarding and sanctioning behaviour, i.e. motivation. In this formulation, end-users appear to be paramount, but if you look closer you'll see that end-users are subordinate to achieving organizational goals. What's more, there's a question about the extent to which you have room to introduce radical new ways of looking at the issue. What if the issue proves to have nothing to do with motivation?

The fifth formulation will probably appeal to designers, just like the third one. This formulation is about discovering and resolving barriers, i.e. an organic process. End-users are again front and centre, and the method is again to be decided. However, a strictly organic approach will not give designers enough options. Organic change assumes a position of 'things happening as they happen' and prefers to look ahead rather than learn from the past. Removing barriers, which is a typically organic intervention, avoids the question of whether or not a fundamentally different way of looking at things is needed, i.e. the reframing. In that case, organic change is not as precise as change through learning, which works towards concrete solutions by doing and thinking about things simultaneously.

CASE STUDY PART 1
CLIMATE ADAPTATION

Our climate is changing and all around the world we're having to prepare for more extreme weather. Citizens' involvement is crucial for this because governments can't do it alone. For instance, everyone paving over their own garden will result in flooding when there's heavy rain. If water can sink into the ground, then streets won't flood and the sewage system won't overflow. Although the specialists in the government have a good idea of which excesses need to be considered and what the promising measures are, they have not yet been able to get enough citizens to take action.

A group of 14 government authorities identified involving citizens in climate adaptation as a challenge that could benefit from a design approach. Working together with civil servants at these public

Fig. 23: Search results on google images for 'klimaatverandering' [translated: climate change].

organizations, I set up a process, the first step of which was formulating the research question. This took more time than expected and taught my team a lot about the context in which we were to set up design processes.

The first research question proposed by the civil servants involved was: how can we better inform people about the importance of climate adaptation? This question suggested a lack of knowledge among the target group. However, when talking about it we discovered that this wasn't such an issue, as the several incidents of extreme weather over the past few years had become engraved in people's minds. What was at play here was the tragedy of the commons: an abstract general interest was being endorsed, while concrete individual behaviour was not being adjusted. A change strategy relying on a systematic approach to get everyone to take measures based on the bigger picture wouldn't be enough.

The second research question that was proposed was for us to focus on the interests at play in the key sectors, e.g. agriculture, and to design something that the public organizations could use to start a dialogue with the sector. This proposal came to a swift conclusion: that's exactly what had been tried in the past few years and also wasn't enough. As such, the

strategy of negotiating was also scratched off the list.

A third and final proposal posited examining how to motivate people to take an adaptive approach to climate change. Subsidies are costly and don't always prove effective. Budgets aren't used a lot, and when they are, it's often by people that may need them the least. As such, investing in a motivating strategy of rewarding (and sanctioning) also didn't prove promising enough to force a breakthrough.

Meanwhile, my team searched 'climate change' in Google Images (see image 23). We saw pictures of polar bears, deserts and chimneys, and what we noticed is that in all these images there was no human dimension. There are no polar bears and deserts in the Netherlands and citizens can't control what comes out of a factory chimney. And besides, the white colour of the smoke that comes out of the chimneys is caused by harmless water vapours and not by (invisible) CO_2.

Together, we concluded that we had to find out what climate change means in the everyday lives of residents in the here and now. This would then allow us to discover a possible new perspective to doing things that would align with the human dimension. It would also allow us to discover what role public organizations could play in this.

So, a combination of a learning and an organic approach to change, which design thinking is particularly suitable for.
As such, the final research question was: what does climate change mean to citizens? This question came with a research schedule and budget, after which we set to work.

DECIDING THE RESEARCH QUESTION TOGETHER

In practice, a formulation for a project is rarely based on just one style of change management. More often than not, there's a combination. A learning approach is difficult for someone from a public organization to manage and as such will come with systematic elements, like agreements about time and money. Negotiating elements will also frequently be added, e.g. progress meetings with a steering committee.

To be able to link a design-thinking process to a research question with enough scope for design, the recommendation is to organize a professional meeting between the designer and the stakeholders at the public organization(s). That said, not all designers will want to comment too much on the research question they're given. "We trust the design process itself will lead to the right design question," is what a designer once said to me. The advantage of that approach is that you can get down to business quickly. The disadvantage, however, is that the scope for design may generally prove too limited and it may also prove difficult, if not impossible, to modify the research question.

As such, I personally prefer to spend additional energy on a good, shared research question before the process begins. There are a number of advantages to this, the first being that I get to work in a project where, ultimately, there is enough scope to design and create. Moreover, researching the question teaches me a lot about the context of the question:

what's already been tried and what doesn't work?
Which flanking systematic and negotiating interventions
are required?

The meeting about the research question also helps to let
the stakeholders know that the process will not only be fun
and inspiring, but may also be uncomfortable because
design thinking requires a way of working that public organizations and the staff involved are not familiar with. The greatest added value of meeting to discuss the research question
is that all stakeholders can explain to their colleagues why
this new approach has been chosen. A meeting about styles
of change management and the specific characteristics of
design thinking offers insights and presents the right language (see also chapter 2 for the tables on what clients ask
and a designer's response).

CASE STUDY PART 2

CLIMATE ADAPTATION

Civil servants were still a little hesitant with the research question "what does climate change mean to citizens?" because they wondered what the knowledge of the specialists involved was then worth. The answer is quite simple: change is only possible when new meaning, empirical understand- ing and negotiating are combined in a synergistic process. In other words, the specialists in this project ensure the design process avoids any pie-in-the- sky thinking, use learning experiences from other experiments, know where the scientific uncertainties are and where additional knowledge can be gained. What's more, they ensure the proposals developed in the design process can be decided on in each of the organizations involved (which the last section in this chapter covers in more detail).

I was happy this hesitation was raised because by talking to the civil serv- ants involved they learned to support the design question and understand what their role in the design process would be. It was clear their detailed knowledge and skills (i.e. empirical understanding) and sensitivity to the complexities of (politics and) govern- ance (i.e. negotiating) would still be of huge importance and that they could serve a design-thinking process.

A good design process provides space for expertise about the subject, the location and the stakeholders.

Key Ideas in This Section

↳ Although a public organization may intend to tackle a social issue using design thinking, that doesn't mean to say that every project formulation or research question offers enough scope for a design approach.

↳ It's wise to spend sufficient time on the research question because this creates the foundation for the collaboration between designers and public organizations.

↳ A professional conversation about preferences in change management styles gives a designer and a representative of the public organization in question the tools to clarify what the traditional way of tackling an issue is and why that doesn't work (anymore)[49]. It also helps to discuss any possible worries about a design-thinking approach.

↳ This conversation is an opportunity for all the stakeholders from the public organization to get a better idea of how they can contribute their knowledge and expertise.

↳ What's more, this conversation also gives all the staff involved at the public organization the language to explain to others why a design process has been chosen and how this differs from the usual ways of working.

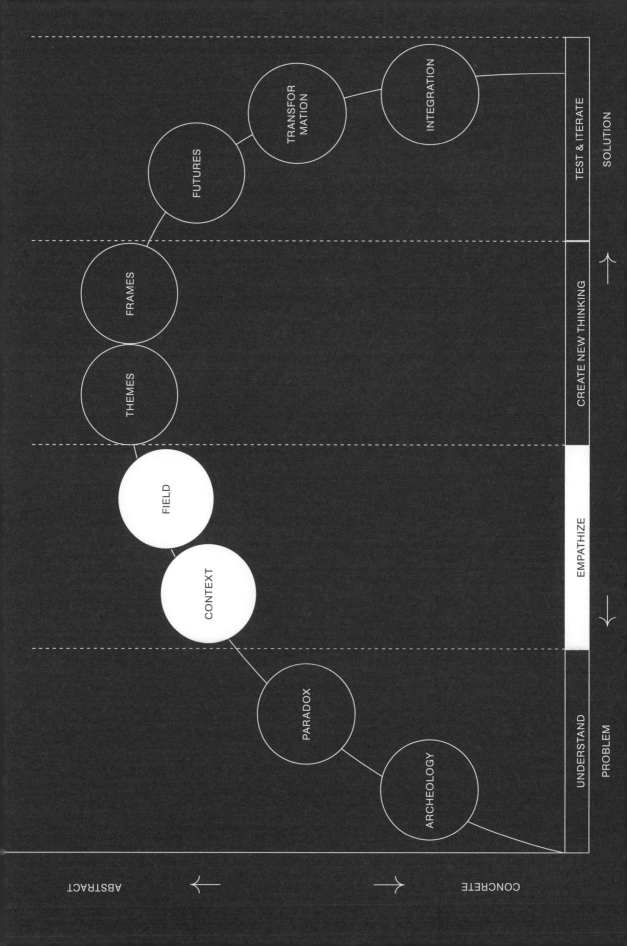

6.2 EMPATHIC RESEARCH

With empathic research, designers try to understand at a deep level what motivates end-users and what holds them back. This appears to seamlessly align with the efforts made by public organizations that say end-users are paramount, regardless of whether they're citizens, entrepreneurs, students, tenants or patients. However, in practice, that's not always the case. And that's because of a rather complex field of tension.

In their work, public sector staff are constantly trying to find a balance between doing things right (according to the system) and doing the right thing (for society). The more expressly the life-world is prioritized, the more difficult it is for that balance to be found. For instance, we were working on a project where designers, farmers and civil servants were looking for solutions to wicked problems in the agricultural sector. At the start of the process, one of the civil servants identified a potential field of tension: "we're asking farmers to work more sustainably and in a way that's more animal-friendly. But if they come up with ideas when working with the designers that require a permit, there's a possibility that we—the government—don't respond to that. We should already come up with something for that now to prevent that from happening."

It pays to examine and discuss the tension between doing things right and doing the right thing. Doing so gives public organizations an idea of the system being part of the problem and the solution, and the urgency and ambition thereof.

Unfortunately, that's sometimes left out and this can pose a risk. After the proposals have been made, a situation can arise in which the representatives of the public sector have to deal with the final proposal, without having a perspective on how to do things. The question then is whether those stakeholders at the public organization are prepared to use the design proposal as the foundation for them independently looking for ways to actually implement it.

Fig. 24: The nine steps of frame innovation – phase 'empathize'.

WAITING ROOMS IN JUVENILE DETENTION FACILITIES[50]

Local county authorities asked Professor Tom Fisher and his team to help redesign the waiting rooms of the county's juvenile detention facilities because fights had begun to break out among the people waiting there. Looking back, the county had hoped that the designers, would come back with waiting-room plans and recommendations for moving furniture, changing the lighting, and maybe putting up a few dividers to separate people and discourage fighting.

Instead, they recommended that the county redesign its juvenile detention process, since no amount of reorganization and redecoration of the waiting rooms would end the fighting, which remained the most visible symptom of a dysfunctional system that frustrated almost everyone involved—those who worked in it as well as those served by it. In making this recommendation, the design team diagrammed the current system, showing where the communication gaps and process breakdowns were occurring. The county had not seen the system visualized in this way, and the designers' diagram led to conversations among people who had not understood how they fit as part of a

larger whole and how they connected to the work of others in ways not immediately apparent.

The design team did not just analyze the situation and help the county visualize its system; it also suggested strategies that would begin to repair the dysfunction.

"This does not always please those in power or those who have a stake in the status quo. The county did not appreciate my colleagues' doing something other than what they had been asked to do, and as a result nothing happened at first. After a while, though, the county's leadership acknowledged the problems with the system and began to act on aspects of the designers' proposal. To their credit, the county leaders overcame their initial annoyance and engaged my colleagues in the redesign of other county systems that were also not working as they should".

Professor Fisher and his team opted to not only look at juvenile prisoners, but also at the people working in the system. Instead of coming up with a simple solution, like modifying the furniture, the client was presented with a more complex problem, i.e. that they had to redesign a dysfunctional detention system. Thanks to the calibre of the designers involved and the client's open mind, this process ultimately led to change.

CONTROLLED CRASH TESTS BETWEEN THE LIFE-WORLD AND THE SYSTEMS

Generally speaking, it's not because of uncooperativeness that clients don't take on designers' recommendations. After all, decision-making in the public sector has to be transparent and public money has to be distributed and spent properly. As such, bureaucratic processes are unavoidable to a certain extent.

Change is only possible if an innovative idea also comes with a new perspective on how to do things that rebalances 'doing things right' with 'doing the right thing'. The design process can play a role in helping find the right balance.

To that end, my team and I organize controlled crash tests between the life-world (of end-users) and the systems (of the organization). A crash test helps to highlight which systems keep the problem alive and ultimately should be redesigned. As part of this process, we look at the core values of the organization in question; after all, its system of rules and protocols is built on these core values. To understand how these core values sustain the issue, we examine which of the core values has an influence on the issue and in what way.

Systems tend
to create
policy-guided
state
volunteers.

RELIABILITY AS A CORE VALUE

Professor Kees Dorst once told me the story about how he'd been approached by a part of the Ministry of Defence that wanted to know how they could become more innovative; they were good at implementing quick improvements, but systematic innovation was proving difficult. When talking to them, Dorst found that 'reliability' was a key core value for the organization. But reliability also meant excluding uncertainty. As such, only proven techniques that had been thoroughly tested were acquired and implemented. This created a procurement strategy that specified everything down to the finest detail.

Dorst introduced the organization to designers and suppliers through a learning and investigative process. This led to better products being bought and at a fraction of the estimated price too. Dorst: "You don't end up having these sorts of conversations based on planning and control; planning and control make you very predictable — something that you don't quite want Defence to be. By taking this explanation of reliability, you lose your flexibility. It's important that that's organized differently, e.g. by not having every single incident lead to a flood of new rules."

An organization's shared core values are a very important starting point in the work I do. What those core values are is something that quickly becomes apparent. One problem, however, is that those core values are often interpreted in a number of different ways. For instance, all staff will acknowledge that transparency is important, but what shape that transparency takes can differ. Every organization also has its compromisers and its hardliners, plus the differences between departments mean there are different viewpoints and differing opinions on preferable and achievable solutions.

My team and I examine this, involving people from different parts of the public organization. We look at what motivates them and what holds them back, learning a lot in the process. We present the different interpretations of the core values and contrast them with the life-world of the end-users, as revealed through our empathic research. This is what we call a 'controlled crash test'.

MAYBOURHOOD

About 15 organizations, including municipalities, the state, a water board and housing associations asked us to come up with a strategy with designers that was both local and customized to encourage participation and make things a success. My team was repeatedly approached with a question that boiled down to this: "how can we ensure that people take more initiative for the quality of life in their own environment?" Each time, our hypothesis was the same: that initiative is already there. In our view, the most important job wasn't to activate citizens; we thought it was more important to connect the public organizations to the existing energy in society.

That's why our first action was to look for the initiatives the government agencies weren't reaching. During our fieldwork, which involved designers and representatives of the public organizations joining forces, we discovered numerous and surprising initiatives. To find out why these initiatives weren't reaching the bureaucratic agencies, we created a theory test for which we took photos of a whole host of examples of local initiatives. We then presented these examples to a large, diverse group of staff, posing the question: "Is this allowed?" (see figure 25). The participants were given a semi-official sheet of answers and we intimated that the result would be included in their next performance review. This proved an interesting experiment each time because nearly every initiative we presented to the group was endorsed by some and met with resistance from others. And both responses could be easily defended.

The test asked the participants straightforward yes/no questions, like "cutting the hedge yourself, is this allowed?" If the municipality doesn't have any money for maintaining public spaces, are you as a citizen allowed to look after the upkeep of the square. Some said they'd be very happy for that to happen, while others said the question was whether citizens knew how to prune responsibly, when that pruning should be done, e.g. in conjunction with the breeding season, and where the garden waste should go.

Mayborhood?
room for initiatives

Enlarging your own handicap parking space.

Is that okay?   ☐ Yes   ☐ No

Mayborhood?
room for initiatives

Trimming the public garden yourself.

Is that okay?   ☐ Yes   ☐ No

Fig. 25:   Four examples of the Mayborhood Theory Exam. (2/2)

Another question was: "keeping an eye on public spaces, is this allowed?" Again, some said it was allowed: "if we're asking people to take responsibility for social safety, then this has to be allowed. Moreover, everyone spends their day filming things on their mobiles and you can also keep an eye on everything from behind your window." The lawyers were the ones to say no: "privacy laws in the Netherlands do not permit this."

"Increasing the size of your parking space, is this allowed?" The pragmatists said yes: "if the owner discusses this with the neighbours and does a good job of the work, then we see no reason to object. This will also go faster than if we were to come by. Also, it saves on costs." The others said no: "in the Netherlands, there's equality before the law. If this person has a larger parking space, then others are also entitled to one."

One final example: "filling in the pavement, is this allowed?" Some again said yes: "if someone wants to spend their time doing that, then that's allowed." Others said no: "If that person lays a paving slab incorrectly and a senior citizens stumbles over it and breaks their hip, then we're responsible."

What this theory test demonstrates is that a public organization has

conflicting roles. They want to encourage initiatives, but are also responsible for the quality of public spaces. Moreover, they are beholden to the law, the guardian of equality before the law and responsible for public safety. Saying 'no' is often seen as more authoritative than saying 'yes'. As a result, participation is designed in practice in such a way that those with the initiatives can only be successful if they behave as 'citizens of the system' or 'policy-guided state volunteers'. In other words, citizens whose initiatives contribute to the political agenda and who conform to the logic of the system.

The way in which core values, such as equality before the law, safety and fit for purpose, are explained has become part of the problem. But these are also the core values that contribute to a reliable public sector, so cannot be casually pushed aside. If you accept the opposite, that will become immediately clear. Who wants a public sector that exudes arbitrary will, takes no responsibility for safety and sets to work in an inefficient and unfocussed manner with no goals?

The question that always arose during each Maybourhood test was: "what does a participation society ask of the public organization?" Of course, there was no immediately clear answer to

In most organizations, it'd only take five minutes to find three people to explain exactly why something is not possible.

this question. The group had a range of conflicting ideas. Whenever this question was put on the table, my team then advised exploring the matter through prototypes and pilot programmes, and the organizations concerned almost always agreed with that suggestion.

During the crash test, we let the different stakeholders in the organization reach their own conclusions. We only facilitate the process by hosting an exploratory meeting that gives all stakeholders insight into how they and their organizations are part of the problem. We usually don't present any conclusions as part of this or any proposals for solutions. At the very most, we present hypotheses.

The crash tests help make the way in which an organization's core values are interpreted part of the problem. This is an important step because how core values are interpreted often impedes change. Or as an employee of a public organization once said to me: "in this organization, it would only take me five minutes to find three people to explain to me exactly why something is not possible."

Making the core values part of the problem also creates the opportunity to ask the following question: "how can the core values become part of the solution?" After carrying out the crash tests between the life-world and the systems, we can ask how we can create the (mental) space for change. An organization is generally then prepared to start investigating that. And the nice thing is that not only has space been created for a system change, but stakeholders also feel challenged in a positive way for the first time to participate in this process.

Key Ideas in This Section

↳   Empathic research examines the life-world of the end-users. The insights from this are then used to examine the core values of the systems world. What are these core values and how are they manifested? Do they sustain the problem and how much scope for change do they offer?

↳   This type of research can be summed up as a controlled crash test, i.e. a confrontation between the life-world of the end-users and the systems of the public organization. The paradoxes and the ambiguity that the empathic research brings to light are identified and embraced. No conclusions are reached yet; at most, hypotheses are formulated.

↳   The crash test challenges public sector staff to discover for themselves in a co-creative process where the systems oppress and what a new perspective on how to do things would look like. How can the organization's core values become part of the solution?

↳   This interim step prevents the organization in question from being 'surprised' at a later stage by proposals suggesting unavoidable system change. Once it's become much clearer how the organization's core values sustain the problem, the stakeholders in the organizations realize that they, too, must look at how they do things. How ready they are to do this is essential for a successful follow-up.

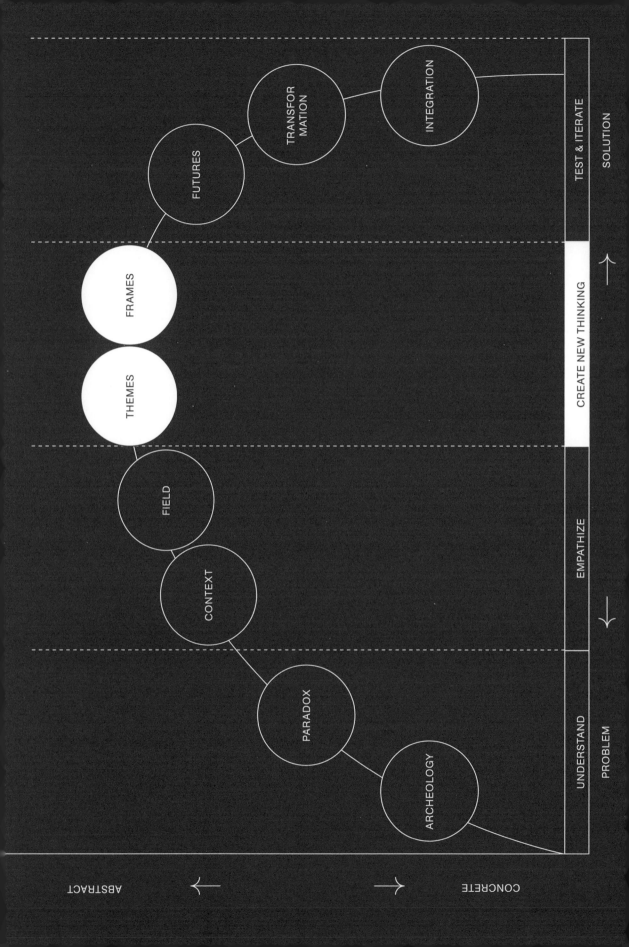

6.3 FRAMING AND REFRAMING

A frame is a perspective from which you look at an issue. Reframing an issue changes the perspective and can lead to whole new ideas. A new frame offers insight into solutions that the old frame had been unable to get on the table.

Reframing an issue is the pièce de résistance of a successful design process. It's the key to innovation and change. Reframing an issue also creates a lot of discussion. What effect does it have on the playing field of the issue? How will the new frame stand up in a political or social debate? What associations do people have with the new frame?

The frame will not only be assessed by stakeholders on how promising it is, but also on what it means for how they do things in practice. Focussing on the new frame's detailed potential means that its significance at a system level can easily be missed. How do you examine the significance and the likelihood of a new frame succeeding at a system level and how do you ensure a new frame is not as susceptible to systemic responses?

HOW DOES THE NEW FRAME RELATE TO THE PLAYING FIELD?

A design process aims to look at things holistically; first diverging and then converging. This means that numerous building blocks are collected in the empathic research phase that don't always lead to a single obvious reframing. In fact, it's preferable to develop several frames and then examine the potential of each one.

Frames are very abstract until you flesh them out. It's only then that you discover who wants to get involved and what proposals they may lead to. The coalition you bring to life will depend on the frame you decide to continue with.

Fig. 26: The nine steps of frame innovation – phase 'create new thinking'.

It's important to understand that not everyone wins with a new frame. There could also be parties who have a certain position because of the old frame and who lose this position because of the reframing. These parties could create a resistance.

Whenever I present frames, every frame has several possible (social) partners. By doing so, the context of each frame is immediately connected to a discussion about the coalition and the working relationships the coalition needs to flesh out the frame (see also chapter 3).

CASE STUDY PART 6

THE A9 LAND TUNNEL

We're going to go back to the A9 project in Amsterdam Zuidoost, the key case study in chapter 4. My team and I were asked how to develop a positive relationship between a six-year-long building project and the people in the surrounding neighbourhood.

During our field research in the area around the building site, we heard a lot of stories about different things, e.g. pride in the local area, health and talent development. This led us to create three frames.

The first was viewing the A9 as the dynamic backdrop against which the project's unique aspects were presented to interested parties from the area and beyond. The second was viewing the A9 as a sort of retreat, where safety on and around the building site was linked to health in the neighbourhood. The third frame was viewing the project as a temporary economy, with a connection between the building project's economic activities and talent development for people in the neighbourhood.

Each frame opens another window to entice interested parties. If you flesh out the 'dynamic backdrop' frame (see figure 27), then tour operators, event organizers, crowd controllers and communications agencies become potential key partners. The municipality's Permits and Tourism departments in particular would have to come on board. If you do the same with the 'retreat' frame, then you quickly end up with the Academic Medical Centre, local municipal

Fig. 27: Artist impression of the frame 'dynamic backdrop'.

A design
frame and
a political
frame are
fundamentally
different
in nature.

health services, local health authorities, GPs, etc. as partners. In terms of the municipality, it's the Public Health & Sport department that's engaged. With the 'temporary economy' frame, schools and training programmes become important. Again, in the case of the municipality, it's the Education and Economy departments that get involved.

When choosing which frame to work out in more detail, the enthusiasm of the intended coalition played a major role, and this enthusiasm was by far the greatest in the 'temporary economy' frame.

HOW DOES A DESIGN FRAME RELATE TO SOCIO-POLITICAL FRAMES?

A design process assumes an open, investigative mentality. This can be forced in the design process, but that's not often the case outside this safe context. In the world of public administration, new frames are not always viewed from a neutral standpoint and evaluated based on their merits. They can also lead to a political game. The newly designed frame then has to battle socio-political frames. Taking a closer look at the political side of public organizations will help to better understand this clash.

At public organizations, directors are the ones with final responsibility for decisions and spending. Chapter 2 already mentioned how directors operate in a permanently unsafe arena. A majority of people in that same area have a different opinion than the director in question. They do everything they can to influence the director's policy. There's nothing essentially wrong with this bureaucratic game; after all, a fierce debate helps to make good decisions. But there's an ugly side to this if negatively framing the other party becomes a goal in itself, e.g. by presenting 'alternative facts'. Opponents put pressure on a director, with the aim of gaining a position of power for themselves. In that case, finding solutions for social problems becomes a secondary objective.

Although the worlds of design thinking and politics use the concept of 'framing', a design frame is often the polar opposite of a political frame. A design process focuses on developing unifying, inclusive frames in which everyone connected to the issue is challenged to become part of the solution. Political framing is a rhetorical technique to turn the debate to your own advantage, often by increasing differences and disqualifying others. That can be done explicitly, but also implicitly. Political frames can also be closely connected to social frames.

DESIGN FRAMES AND SOCIO-POLITICAL FRAMES

The pro-life movement was established by people who are against abortion. They could have called themselves the anti-abortion movement, but instead chose pro-life. This framing is a particularly effective way of influencing the debate because if someone who opposes abortion is called pro-life, what do you call someone who supports abortion? Anti-life? A rather unpleasant label, so supporters of freely available abortion went looking for a more positive frame for themselves. They called themselves pro-choice, thereby classifying the others as anti-choice — another unpleasant label.

In the end, the battle between these sorts of frames leads to a wider gap between the parties in question and not to the bridge-building that could help progress the issue. There are numerous examples of different frames fighting for dominance, both in the political world and in society, and they're always easy to spot.

Things get more complicated when there's a political or social consensus about a particular frame, and that frame is preventing the issue from being resolved. This isn't always the work of clever spin doctors; this situation arises in the difficult-to-define interplay between society, media and politics.

For example, a national Dutch newspaper published an appeal by scientists to politicians and society at [50] large to be more careful with figures on crime and ethnicity[51]. The scientists identified that overrepresentation of certain ethnic groups in crime statistics was creating a frame that crime among parts of the population with a migrant background was an ethnic issue. The scientists claimed, however, that when corrected for social position, the figures showed that the overrepresentation of people with a different ethnic background was no longer significant.

According to the scientists, the problem is not an ethnic one, but a social one – not a trivial difference. The frames of 'crime is an ethnic problem' and 'crime is a social problem' both lead to entirely different interventions.

People who view crime as an ethnic problem quickly conclude that people with a different ethnic background do not respect 'our' culture. In that case, social interventions don't appease them. The fact that their preference for repressive measures is part of the reason the problem has become such a tough one is simply dismissed. Whenever a design frame leads to proposals aimed at improving social standing, the greater the likelihood of them being set aside for being too 'soft', making the design frame, de facto, unusable.

A design process can come up with some wonderful frames that, on paper, connect and invite parties to become part of the solution. But when a design frame like that comes up against political or social frames, it can get the worst of it and become unusable. To be able to estimate whether a design frame will survive once it's exposed to political or social frames, you first need to analyze the dominant frames. There's nothing wrong then if a design frame aligns with these dominant frames; in fact, a design frame and a political frame can then enhance each other. If that's not the case, then there may be reason to reinterpret the design frame in a smart way so that it does become politically and socially feasible. Connecting design frames and socio-political frames, where end-users' wellbeing is paramount, is no easy task and requires all stakeholders to be able to establish a process that addresses the challenging situation.

A design frame
will only be
useful if it's
politically and
socially feasible.

DESIGN FRAMES AND SOCIO-POLITICAL FRAMES WHAT ASSOCIATIONS CAN A NEW FRAME EVOKE?

Sometimes a design frame may look like something that has already received a negative response. In that case, there's a significant chance that there are visible and invisible mechanisms built into the system that will see another negative response. This undermines the feasibility of the design frame.

I've learned to identify and explicate these mechanisms in good time. Before a frame has been fleshed out into concrete proposals, schedules and budgets, I first ask whether the organization has had any experience with proposals like these. What are the written and unwritten rules that form part of this? Opening these up to discussion quickly clarifies whether the new frame is viable and under what conditions.

CASE STUDY
MOVING A BRIDGE

I was asked to think about moving a 200-metre-long bridge. This bridge had been built close to its final home, so it had to be moved at a certain point — something that obviously wouldn't go unnoticed. There was a concern that this move would draw a huge audience. People were concerned about dangerous situations arising because of the unsupervised influx of interested parties wanting to watch the move. My team was asked to think about a good process for moving the bridge.

We understood the curiosity of those in the neighbouring area. Imagine seeing such a huge bridge being transported across the area where you live and/or work. We reframed this into a piece of theatre. What story do you want to tell, what will the good vantage points be, how will you keep up the suspense? And of course: how will you ensure people can reach the area and how will you look after the guests? My team, which included specialists from a large site-specific theatre, developed a plan that was approved by the contractor. That certainly wasn't an easy task because we received new details about the move nearly every day, which meant our plan had to be as flexible as possible.

In the end, we got all parties at all levels to agree. And then....nothing. After we delivered our plan, hidden forces emerged that I hadn't foreseen. People started asking how the idea would reflect on the organization. Would people be put out by the fact that something festive was being organized, while the neighbouring area had been dealing with the construction and disruption for some time? Would critical questions be asked about how much the event was costing?

Before I knew what was going on, our idea was totally ripped apart. In the end, the road was closed off to the public, only a small group of guests were invited to watch and a live webcam feed was set up for other interested parties — a feed on which you couldn't see anything because the move was done at night.

Looking back, I can now say there were no problems during the move and our exhaustive plan wasn't really necessary. On the other hand, for minimal additional cost the neighbouring area could have been invited to be involved in this extraordinary event, so that's something of a missed opportunity.

So why did a plan that enjoyed widespread support and enthusiasm end up in someone's drawer? What I'd heard but underestimated was that there'd been major social upset before about the cost of a ceremonial opening for a similar project. This not only resulted in the actual budgets for events being slashed — our proposal was still within these lower budgets by the way — it also resulted in people being far less open to such events being organized. If something was being organized, it had to exude frugality. Our plan had in fact aimed to achieve the best possible appearance using minimal resources, which ultimately spelled its death.

Key Ideas in This Section

↳ Reframing is the key to finding a solution for a wicked problem. It introduces a new way of looking at the issue and offers a new perspective on solutions that had previously been out of the picture.

A frame that's been well formulated from a design perspective may, in practice, be vulnerable. As such, it's important to find out whether the design frame is politically and socially feasible. If it isn't, the proposals stemming from it won't be accepted either.

↳ To get a sense of the feasibility of a design frame, ask yourself the following questions:
↳ How will the design frame change the playing field? Will it allow for a new coalition to be formed? Will there be parties who lose their position and will they fight back?
↳ How does the design frame relate to the dominant political and social frames around the issue?
↳ What experiences have people had with the frame? What associations does it evoke?

↳ If the design frame is vulnerable, it should be strengthened by building the necessary coalition, increasing the overlap with political and social frames and/or making negative associations manageable.

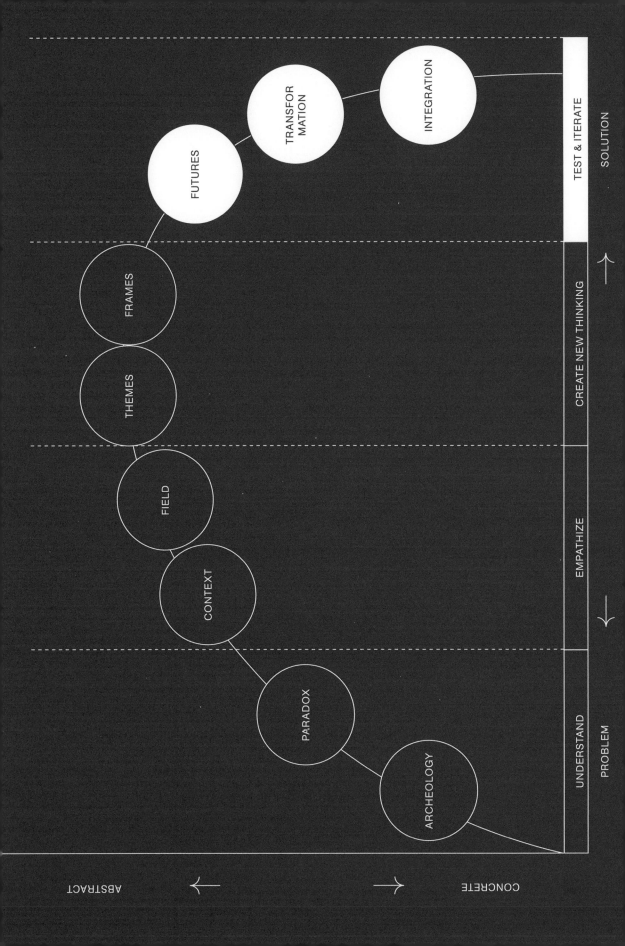

6.4 PROTOTYPING

In a design-thinking process, you're continuously testing ideas, insights and hypotheses. But the most important tests happen in the phase that follows the development of a new frame. A good frame opens the window to promising new ideas, but also to ideas that are as yet unproven. Prototyping helps to quickly test these ideas and to discover in short iterative steps whether there are forces influencing these ideas and how these forces can be handled. At the end of the day, this helps implementation go more smoothly.

Prototyping is a proven method to achieve effective proposals in a short and efficient manner. However, while public organizations are enthusiastic about empathic research (where end-users are placed front and centre) and reframing, they're a little reluctant when it comes to prototyping. I've been surprised about this more than once. After all, you often read about large projects by public organizations getting completely out of hand because, in practice, they're dealing with complex and expensive hiccups. And then there are the other times when people have continued to work on something that proved impossible to get off the ground. It seems that taking a project-based approach alone, i.e. thinking things through properly to deliver a proposal and then structurally implementing it, doesn't work for public organizations. So how liberating would it be to do some prototyping during a complex project, like designers do? Why the reluctance? To get a better understanding of this, this section will outline the systematic resistance against prototyping that can be found at public organizations and how to handle this.

Fig. 28: The nine steps of frame innovation – phase 'test and iterate'.

PUBLIC ORGANIZATIONS AND PROTOTYPING

I spoke to Professor Ad van Berlo[52] about the stance public organizations have on prototyping.

"The big difference between government authorities and designers is that government authorities first think through policy thoroughly and then implement it. Designers lay down the first concept and take small iterative steps to improve that proposal or come up with a new proposal if the first one doesn't work well enough.

Both approaches can be successful if you implement them at the right time. What I see now, however, is that in a fluid environment, where structure is being built in a chaotic environment, government authorities are still holding steadfastly to traditional linear structures to find new policy.

At the same time, government authorities realize they need something different. This is leading to interesting concepts, like the Lean startup. But with the exception of a few experiments, most government authorities don't yet believe in iterative models for policy-making. That's understandable too. Say, for example, you introduce a new tax system and then in the following period start explicitly closing the gaps based on experience. This will be a tough story to sell, politically speaking. Ironically enough, this is how things often go.

The government and society at large are also affected by things like this. Take new market parties like AirBnB and Uber, for example. The government is trying to formulate a standpoint, but hasn't found one yet, and as a result these parties can just do their thing, with both positive and negative consequences. I think it's astonishing this hasn't been turned into an experiment, where after one year the government evaluates whether the policy has worked, and does so again the following year."

PROTOTYPING CREATES VULNERABILITY

Chapter 2 already talked about how directors of public organizations operate in a permanently unsafe arena. There's a constant battle for (positional) power and as a result the scope for not knowing something is limited. If something doesn't go well the first time, there's always the possibility that the director responsible will be dismissed by opponents as someone who's incompetent or inconsistent or who is frivolous with taxpayers' money.

That dynamic of the unsafe arena of public administration filters down to public organizations because even if a director hasn't been personally actively associated with a project, in the end they're the person who has final responsibility. If people get upset, then this also filters down to the director. Public organization staff are very familiar with these mechanisms. This is referred to as having a sensitivity to the complexities of (politics and) governance. This explains the preference for structured change in the public sector. This, after all, is the most predictable, manageable and focussed approach. This translates to a systemic resistance to prototyping.

By the way, I don't want to suggest that there's no room for experimenting in the public sector. Public sector staff are always successfully making space for pilots[53] or learning and development projects. But, as a rule, this is done as part of strategic issues. There's little room for experimenting in urgent operational issues. In my experience, the openness of public sector staff to experimenting is decreasing as the urgency to develop innovative proposals is increasing—that's quiet some paradox. People are being pressured to solve a problem and that pressure is only increasing with each 'failure'.

THE VARIABLES AND CONCEPTS
TO BE TESTED ARE NOT NEUTRAL

A second systemic resistance to prototyping can be explained by way of the fact that the ideas to be tested may be socially sensitive ideas. Regardless of whether a design process is being conducted to address a strategic or an operational issue, prototyping is the stage at which the design process becomes visible to the outside world. Serious ideas are put on the table for the first time; these are examined and people asked to relate to them. Sometimes these are ideas that nobody can resist, but if the ideas are socially sensitive this may create a dynamic that's difficult for designers to manage.

CASE STUDY PART 1

THE DIY-CHICKEN

The agricultural sector is an important economic pillar in the Dutch province of Noord–Brabant. But it's also a sector in crisis, economically, socially and ecologically speaking. I supported the province in their coalition with farmers, designers and other players in the food supply chain in the Landbouw Innovatie Campus [literally: Agriculture Innovation Campus] initiative[54], which seeks to find innovative new solutions for this agricultural crisis.

One of the subjects we tackled was the meat production process. As a society, we consume more meat than is sustainably responsible. Consumers set high requirements in terms of animal welfare and the quality of the meat, but also in terms of price, which

in the end is often the deciding factor. Farmers should responsibly produce meat that is both animal–friendly and inexpensive. There are very limited options for this combination.

One of the concepts that was developed as part of the Landbouw Innovatie Campus was the 'doehetzelfkip' (literally: the DIY chicken, see figures 29, 30 and 31)[55]. Using this concept, we examined if it was possible to give back responsibility for the entire meat production process, including butchery, to consumers and if so, how, and also what this might do to consumption patterns.

The 'doehetzelfkip' is a cage with three fertilized eggs inside, an incubator, food for nine weeks, ground cover for the coop and the tools to butcher the chicken, i.e. a club to knock out the chicken, a killing cone and a knife. The cage is an ingenious little design that first serves as a nest for the chickens, then turns into a chicken coop and finally can be used as a chopping block.

Farmers were enthusiastic about the idea and keen to start testing with consumers. We realized that butchering the chickens would be a particularly sensitive social issue and asked ourselves how the Landbouw Innovatie Campus as a public organization could get involved. We thought the issue was very relevant, but did we want to facilitate a project where animals die? On the other hand, 28 million chickens are butchered every year in the province of Noord-Brabant. Plus, private individuals in the Netherlands are legally permitted to butcher chickens on a small scale. We realized we could only look into the responsibility for meat production, if the discussion didn't end up being about why the research was needed. This required an ethical and well-substantiated experiment.

Technically speaking, prototyping can be done very safely. But because the process is visible, the conversation can unintentionally shift towards a social and political discourse. It's good to realize that the designer has little control, if any, if a conversation shifts to a different discourse. A political or social discussion can provide input for an iterative step, as design prefers, but it can also lead to the design process itself becoming the topic of discussion.

As such, to maintain a sense of calm in the prototyping process, it's advisable to think about what 'failures' you should consider during prototyping and whether or not these will be acceptable from a political or social standpoint. Also, it's important to review all variables with a healthy dose of sensitivity to the complexities of (politics and) governance, and to ensure that the choices made can be explained.

The political
feasibility
of the prototyping
process should
be considered,
as well as the
feasibility of
the proposals
the process
produces.

THE DIY-CHICKEN

The province of Noord-Brabant was familiar with design thinking and prototyping. A decision was made to take the 'doehetzelfkip' a step further and work towards an experiment with three consumers. This was done with the utmost care for animal wellbeing and public perception.

The designers first conducted a careful experiment with nine chickens, in preparation for which they reviewed what the Dutch law says about private individuals butchering animals and learned as much as possible about keeping chickens. Under expert supervision, they learned how to butcher chickens. This expert was also involved in writing the manual for the 'doehetzelfkip'.

This was followed by a search for people to participate in the trial. Participants were asked about their motivations and customized plans devised for their supervision, where measures relating to the wellbeing of the chickens were paramount. This would ensure that the participants could seek advice and, if necessary, support with any action they had to undertake. One of the conditions of being able to participate was that the butchering would not be turned into a (media) event.

Despite all our hard work to do everything in the most animal-friendly manner possible and with the utmost integrity, something unexpected happened. One of our project followers – someone who was positive and curious about it – asked in passing why "the province had opted" for a fast-growing breed of chicken. These are chickens that grow so fast they develop lesions relatively quickly. To be clear, this is a breed of chicken that's the most popular in meat production; supermarkets are full of meat from these chickens. The province sets great store by animal welfare, and the person asking the question couldn't see how these two things could go together. I understood this, but realized that the choice of chicken breed in our trial was being viewed as a final decision, supported by a public administration, when in fact it was neither.

The designers had chosen this breed of chicken because they wanted the trial to be as real as possible. Moreover, they were able to get fertilized eggs from this breed of chicken very easily. If the trial participants were to say they didn't like the fast-growing chickens (or didn't think they tasted nice) that could be an argument to discuss the choice of breed and

choose a different one for the next
version of the 'doehetzelfkip'. But you
have to be allowed to take this next
iterative step.

THREE RULES OF THUMB
FOR PROTOTYPING

The process of prototyping and the choice of variables to
test can lead to opposing political or social forces. Often,
this results in a defensive response from the public organization involved: de-escalating, scaling back, calming down. In
short: the curtains come down. It goes without saying that
this doesn't help in the search for effective solutions. This
response can also be avoided. Taking the right actions creates the quiet space required for the necessary trials. To
achieve this, I have three rules of thumb.

RULE 1: DIFFERENTIATE BETWEEN
RISK AND UNCERTAINTY

There are a whole host of processes at public organizations
designed to avoid mistakes, e.g. risk management. This
process collates all possible risks from different points of
view and then draws up measures to manage these risks. As
such, risk management is a great help with realizing projects
on time and within budget, and preventing any (bureaucratic)
hassle.

Prototyping, however, is not about risks; it's about uncertainty. "Uncertainty is a situation where there is a lack of probabilities. There is no prior data on how solutions might per-
form, future outcomes are not known and can therefore not
be measured. The chance of success can be anything from
0 to 100%. Running experiments at an early stage is really a
systematic way of turning uncertainty into a set of probabilities that, in turn, can be experimented with and managed

It's not the result of the design process that most often hinders implementation, but the lack of clarity about the choices that are made.

within a more defined scope. In this sense, policy initiatives can be used as learning opportunities to deal with uncertainty in ways that create a set of useful probabilities to close the gap between uncertainty and risk."[56]

Unfortunately, uncertainty is usually dealt with as one of the risks to be managed. This misinterpretation is a little frustrating because prototyping in fact helps to minimize uncertainty—something that cannot be done if you avoid uncertainty altogether. That said, there's nothing wrong with properly taking stock of risks, as long as you also keep a close eye on what uncertainty you're investigating.

RULE 2: DIFFERENTIATE BETWEEN GOOD AND BAD FAILURES

Creating space for prototyping is more than just acknowledging that you may learn more from your mistakes than from successful experiments. It's about making it very clear why you're conducting a particular experiment. This requires a coherent narrative that explains the problem, the insights you've gained from the end-users (including the paradoxes sustaining the issue) and what frame this has led to. This precedes the question of what you want to learn during the prototyping stage, what uncertainties you want to minimize and what trial you've come up with for that purpose. As such, it helps to decide what your good and bad failures are before you start the trial. A bad failure is one where the effect could have been predicted and the tester learns nothing. A good failure is one that provides insight into the uncertain effects of a proposal; this type of failure can be explained.

RULE 3: CONSIDER POLITICAL FEASIBILITY

It's important at all stages of design thinking to consider the political feasibility of what you're doing, especially at the prototyping stage because that's the stage of the design process that things becomes concrete and visible. As such, this means that the political feasibility of the prototyping process should be considered, as should the feasibility of the proposals the process produces.

The prototyping process can be achieved if it can be communicated, if it's very easy to explain why certain trials are being carried out. What problem are you tackling and what do you expect to learn from the trials?

In this case, it's wise to continue to keep an eye on the feasibility of the proposals that follow the prototyping phase. This will become politically achievable if they can contribute to a solution for the issue in question. On the one hand, that's a matter of content: does the proposal work? But there's a process side to the matter too: what will everyone's role be? What's required in terms of time, money and capacity to be able to implement the proposal and can these resources be organized? In short: can the people in the organization implement or facilitate the proposal, and do they want to?

Ensuring a design proposal can be achieved and communicated in a bureaucratic fashion is itself a process. It's important to understand that during this process there's generally very little opportunity for discussion with the director of the public organization. Their staff are often a good sounding board for the designer, but they can't always follow every step of the design process. As such, when presenting a proposal, you should pay attention to the content of the proposal and the process that was used to get there. A director I spoke to summarized it as follows: "to be able to accept the outcomes of a design process at a bureaucratic level, a director of a public organization must be able to have an overview of the content and the consequences. They must also be able to explain what the process was that led to these proposals. That's why a director should be involved in the creation of a proposal. At the same time, this is difficult to achieve because of people's jam-packed diaries. As such, it's important to document the design process properly, so that everyone understands how you reached the proposal."

THE DIY-CHICKEN

So what happened next with the 'doehetzelfkip'? The first trial with three participants went well; they felt responsible for the chicken's welfare and wanted to ensure they were butchered without any unnecessary suffering. Although the instructions provided for butchering the chickens were clear, the participants went looking for additional information and experience.

Of the three participants in the trial, two ultimately butchered the chickens themselves — in one instance under the supervision of a neighbour. One of the participants brought the chickens to the poulterer. All of the participants said after the trial that they made other, more sustainable choices when shopping, i.e. they bought less and better meat.

These insights led to the 'doehetzelfkip' version 2.0. While the first trial had been conducted behind closed doors, so to speak, the second trial involving six households was widely publicized. This generated articles in a number of national newspapers, reports on national TV and radio, including an extensive and extraordinarily captivating interview on one of the country's most important news programmes with one the

farmers involved in the project. In the interview, the farmer was very open about how the ambiguity of butchering animals (i.e. you care about them, but you still have them killed in the end) affects him and how he wants to speak to consumers about this. Nearly 200 people said they'd be interested to take part in trial no.2.

What was striking about this is that barely a bad word was spoken in the media, not even on social media. The 'doehetzelfkip' had managed to get rid of one important uncertainty: large numbers of consumers were prepared to become part of the problem and part of the solution. That's a significant development in this complex social issue that will be addressed in more detail in the next stage of the project. Landbouw Innovatie Campus is the public organization that facilitated this development[57].

The only resistance to this project worth mentioning came from the political arena. The Party for the Animals[58], which in 2018 holds five seats in the Dutch parliament, thought the project was inappropriate and asked questions in parliament. The Minister of Agriculture, Nature & Food Quality had her civil servants critically review the project and then said she was positive about it and had no reason to take any measures. Once it was clear their dissatisfaction wouldn't see any political consequence, the Party for the Animals decided to make a moral appeal to the participants in the trial to allow the party to adopt their chickens, so that they could take care of them and prevent them from being butchered. None of the participants accepted this offer. The design team's invitation to the Party of the Animals to meet with the farmers and the participants to discuss the project was not accepted either. Despite a few pointed press releases and statements on social media, there was barely any social traction, at which point the Party for the Animals let the matter drop.

Fig. 31: One of the families participating in the doehetzelfkip project.

Key Ideas in This Section

↳ Prototyping helps to minimize the uncertainty about the effectiveness of a proposal. This is done in small iterative steps. Most public organizations have very little experience with this.

↳ Prototyping often faces resistance at public organizations because it's felt that it's difficult to combine with the key core values that public organizations have, such as purpose, efficiency and predictability. Experimenting and as such making mistakes can lead to a political vulnerability.

↳ Prototyping makes the design process very visible. Criticism from the political arena or society can make the prototyping process difficult to manage. As such, consider in advance which variables are part of the trial and which political and social discussion these could incite.

↳ To create enough scope for the prototyping process, there are three important recommendations: 1) avoid misconceptions about risk and uncertainty, 2) differentiate between good and bad failures, and 3) consider the political feasibility of the final proposals.

NOTES

1 In this book, the term 'public sector' refers to government authorities and semi-governmental authorities such as housing associations, healthcare institutes, educational institutes, the energy sector, etc. These are organizations with a legal duty and a clear public interest, and which in general get a substantial part of their funding from public resources.

2 I borrowed this description from change management expert Hans Vermaak (www.hansvermaak.nl).

3 The traits "open, dynamic and networked" are from: Dorst, K. (2015). Frame Innovation—Create New Thinking by Design. Cambridge, USA: The MIT Press.

4 Depending on the case study, 'end-users' refers to citizens, students, patients, passengers, etc.

5 Kees Dorst is Professor of Design Innovation at the Faculty of Transdisciplinary Innovation, University of Technology Sydney.

6 Papanek, V. (1971). Design for the Real World: Human Ecology and Social Change, New York, USA: Pantheon Books.

7 www.socialdesignonderzoek.nl Schaminée, A. J. M., Kuitenbrouwer, K., & Goudswaard, T. (2014, 14 October). SOCIALDESIGNFORWICKEDPROBLEMS. Consulted via https://issuu.com/hetnieuweinstituut/docs/sdfwp_english.

8 Baan, W. (2013, 17 May). Richard Buchanan being interviewed about his four orders of design. Consulted on 1 March 2018: http://www.wilbertbaan.nl/2013/05/17/richard-buchanan-being-interviewed-about-his-4-orders-of-design. Richard Buchanan is associated with the Weatherhead School of Management as a professor of design, management and information systems.

9 Korsten, A. (2008, 14 December). Conceptualizing through policy framing (Dutch). Consulted on 1 March 2018: http://www.arnokorsten.nl/PDF/Beleid/Conceptualisering20door20framing.pdf.

10 Nair, H. (2017). Global, regional, and national disease burden estimates of acute lower respiratory infections due to respiratory syncytial virus in young children in 2015: a systematic review and modelling study. The Lancet, 390 (10098), 946-958.

11 Dorst, K. (2015). Frame Innovation—Create New Thinking by Design. Cambridge, USA: The MIT Press.

12 Based on Hans Vermaak in At Your Service? Algera, K. (2011). At your service? (Dutch) Amsterdam, the Netherlands: No Academy.

13 Fisher, T. (2017, 2 August). Rethinking Design Thinking. Consulted on 1 October 2017: https://www.huffingtonpost.com/entry/rethinking-design-thinking_us_589b504ce4b061551b3e066a?guccounter=1.

14 Dorst, K. (2015). Frame Innovation—Create New Thinking by Design. Cambridge, USA: The MIT Press.

15 Léon de Caluwé, Hans Vermaak, Learning to change—A guide for organizational change agents, Sage, 2003; H. Vermaak & L. de Caluwé, 'The colours of change—revisited. Situating and describing the theory and its practical applications'; draft manuscript to be published in: R. Shani & D. Noumair (eds.) (2018); Vermaak, H. (2015). Plezier beleven aan taaie vraagstukken (Dutch). Deventer, the Netherlands: Vakmedianet.

16 The US television series House of Cards illustrates the bad side of this style of change management.

17 www.socialdesignonderzoek.nl Schaminée, A. J. M., Kuitenbrouwer, K., & Goudswaard, T. (2014, 14 October). SOCIALDESIGNFORWICKEDPROBLEMS. Consulted: https://issuu.com/hetnieuweinstituut/docs/sdfwp_english.

18 Based on table 3.2 in De Caluwé, L. en H. Vermaak (1999) Leren Veranderen (Dutch). Deventer, The Netherlands: Vakmedianet

19 Private communication, 20 April 2017.

20 Hans Vermaak, Schaminée, A. J. M., Kuitenbrouwer, K., & Goudswaard, T. (2014, 14 October). SOCIALDESIGNFORWICKEDPROBLEMS. Consulted via https://issuu.com/hetnieuweinstituut/docs/sdfwp_english.

21 De Jong, M. (2016). Coalition Planning Directive, collective and connective ways of working on the interface of established institutions and individual aspirations >>. Spatial Planning in a Complex Unpredictable World of Change, Gert de Roo and Luuk Boelens (eds.) 1, 260-312. Martine de Jong is a senior consultant at Twynstra Gudde.

22 The project was conducted by a team led by my colleague, Jaap Warmenhoven, senior consultant at Twynstra Gudde.

23 De Jong, M. (2018). Tweebenig spelen (Dutch). In M. de Jong, H. Bakker, & F. Robeert (eds.), Tweebenig samen werken (pp. 8-62). Deventer, the Netherlands: Vakmedianet.

24 Jan Boelen is a Belgian critic and curator of contemporary art and design exhibitions. He has been head of the Master Department Social Design at Design Academy Eindhoven (Netherlands) since 2010.

25 Thanks to Mensink, W. (2015, 20 April). Systeem- en leefwereld: hoe de kloof te dichten (Dutch). Consulted on 12 March 2018: https://www.socialevraagstukken.nl/systeem-en-leefwereld-hoe-de-kloof-te-dichten/

For more information, please refer to Habermas, J. (1981). The Theory of Communicative Action: Volume 2: Lifeword and System: A Critique of Functionalist Reason (Originally published as Theorie des kommunikativen Handelns, Band 2: Zur Kritik der funktionalistischen Vernunft,). Consulted: http://www.academia.edu/2338261/

The_Theory_of_Communicative_Action_Volume_2_Lifeword_and_System_A_Critique_of_Functionalist_Reason.

26 The project and programme definitions come from: Kor, R., & Wijnen, G. (2007). 59 Checklists for Project and Programme Managers. Aldershot, UK: Gower.

27 Private communication, e-mail from Marlieke Kieboom, 8 February 2018.

28 Fisher, R., Urry, W., & Patton, B. (1981). Getting to Yes. London, UK: Penguin.

29 There are numerous toolkits available for empathic research, e.g. Stickdorn, M., & Schneider, J. (2010). Now This Is Service Design Thinking. Amsterdam, the Netherlands: BIS Publishers contains a number of them outlined in a transparent and accessible manner, e.g. the 5 WHYs, shadowing, making customer journeys.

30 Wesselink, M. (2010). Handboek strategisch omgevingsmanagement (Dutch). Deventer, the Netherlands: Vakmedianet.

31 Wesselink, M. (2010). Handboek strategisch omgevingsmanagement (Dutch). Deventer, the Netherlands: Vakmedianet.

32 [Website Buurbouw]. Consulted on 4 May 2018: www.buurbouw.nl.

33 [Website Stadshout]. Consulted on 4 May 2018: http://stadshout.nu/.

34 [Website Amsterbammetje]. Consulted on 4 May 2018: http://amsterbammetje.nu/.

35 Private communication with Frans de Kock (project leader) and Lammert Postma (stakeholder manager) of Rijkswaterstaat, 5 March 2018.

36 Caribbean FM, 25 November 2017, from 11:15 a.m. to 11:45 a.m.

37 In this chapter, I have gratefully referred to David, O. (2015). Macht! Van instinct tot integriteit (Dutch) (3rd ed.). Amsterdam, the Netherlands: Mediawerf en De Caluwé, L., Kor, R., & Wijnen, G. (2005). Essenties van organiseren, managen en veranderen (Dutch). Schiedam, the Netherlands: Scriptum.

38 Northouse, P. (1997). Leadership. London, UK: Sage.

39 David, O. (2015). P. 235 Macht! Van instinct tot integriteit (Dutch) (3rd ed.). Amsterdam, the Netherlands: Mediawerf.

40 [Website Dutch Design Week]. Consulted: www.ddw.nl.

41 This list is not restrictive and the sources of power can be applied alongside each other. Moreover, these sources of power are not exclusive to designers. As a rule, design courses develop these sources of power more than other course do.

42 Fides Lapidaire, 23 January 2018.

43 Interview, 10 July 2017.

44 [PaPa Platform] consulted 30 september 2018: www.papaplatform.com

45 [The Ocean Cleanup]. Consulted on 27 July 2018: https://www.theoceancleanup.com/.

46 [Mine Kafon]. Consulted on 27 July 2018: http://minekafon.org/.

47 [The Fair Phone]. Consulted on 27 July 2018: https://www.fairphone.com/en/.

48 Interview with Joost Voerman, 22 August 2017

49 This is a conversation that fits perfectly in the archaeology step of frame innovation (Dorst, K. (2015). Frame Innovation—Create New Thinking by Design. Cambridge, USA: The MIT Press).

50 Fisher, T. (2016) Designing Our Way to a Better World Minneapolis USA: University of Minnesota Press, pages VIII - X.

51 Jennissen, R., Dagevos, J., & Engbersen, G. (2016, 6 February). Migranten crimineler? Niet selectief shoppen in onze cijfers (Dutch). NRC, 22.

52 Ad van Berlo is the general director of the VanBerlo Group design agency and a part-time professor of the entrepreneurial design of intelligent systems Eindhoven University of Technology in the Netherlands.

53 There is a subtle difference between a prototype and a pilot. There are several definitions out there. What these definitions have in common is that a prototype is generally a faster, lighter way of trialling parts of the whole and a pilot tests the whole system, takes up more work and is more expensive.

54 [Website Landbouw Innovatie Campus]. Consulted on 27 July 2018: http://www.landbouwinnovatiecampus.nl/.

55 This concept was developed by Vera Bachrach and Sadcha Landshoff. [Experimental production house Jansen Jansen Landshoff en Bachrach]. (http://www.jansenjansenbachrachenlandshoff.nl/).

56 Quagiotto, G., Leurs, B., & Christiansen, J. (2017, 6 March). Towards an experimental culture in government: reflections on and from practice. Consulted on 15 July 2017: https://www.nesta.org.uk/blog/towards-an-experimental-culture-in-government-reflections-on-and-from-practice/.

57 https://www.partyfortheanimals.nl/

58 The project could be followed on: www.doehetzelfkip.nl (Dutch)

FIGURES

CREDITS

Fig. 1: Model is based on the work of Richard Buchanan.
Fig. 2: Model is based on a figure in 'conceptualizing through policy framing' by Arno Korsten (2008)
Fig. 3, 21, 22, 24, 26 and 28:
         Model is based on the nine steps of Kees Dorst's frame innovation. I added the categorization 'understand, empathize, create new thinking and test & iterate'. The figure was inspired by a representation of the nine steps of frame innovation by VanBerlo.
Fig. 4, 5, 9:
         The signs for the detour were co-created by local secondary school students of Arte College. © Twynstra Gudde / Rijkswaterstaat.
Fig. 6: Is closely based on tables published by Hans Vermaak en Léon de Caluwé.
Fig. 7 and 8:
         Are inspired by the work of Léon de Caluwé.
Fig. 10: I got a helping hand from Dick Rijken for this figure.
Fig. 12: Picture by Manon van Hoeckel.
Fig. 13: Picture by Rijkswaterstaat.
Fig. 16: Picture by Rijkswaterstaat.
Fig. 17: Design Johanna Koelman Bastiaan Heus 2012.
Fig. 18: Drawing by Kees Dorst.
Fig. 19: © PAPA/Lino Hellings Ramallah Palestine 19 April 2014.
Fig. 20: Image made by Tabo Goudswaard.
Fig. 25: Pictures by André Schaminée and Tabo Goudswaard.
Fig. 27: Image made by Anja Grooten, © Twynstra Gudde.
Fig. 29: By JJBL.
Fig. 30: Pictures by Guus Kaandorp, drawing by Johannes Verwoerd.
Fig. 31: By Willeke Machiels Fotografie - Landbouw Innovatie Campus.

Epilogue

The stories and insights I've shared in this book are inseparable from the people and projects that have crossed my path. I'm very grateful to many people for the practical experience I've gained and which forms the basis of this book

I'd first like to thank my business partners, Jaap Warmenhoven and Tabo Goudswaard. Together, we've spent the past decade on a wonderful journey of discovery that can keep on going, as far as I'm concerned.

Secondly, I'd like to thank the successive directors of Twynstra Gudde who supported and challenged me from the very beginning: Carol Lemmens, Marcel de Rooij and Joost Voerman. I'd also like to thank Peter Groeneveld, a partner at Twynstra Gudde, who led me away from some internal organizational cliffs in the early days.

Many of my insights have been gained from working on projects. These insights would have never existed had I not had the time to reflect with my clients and the designers involved. It's impossible for me to name everyone here, but I'd still like to mention a few people who played an important role in the central case studies.

Tabo Goudswaard and Vera Winthagen (on behalf of VanBerlo) worked on the Best Detour of the Netherlands in chapter 2. Lex Dekker was our client. The Social Support Act in chapter 3 is a project by Jaap Warmenhoven. He worked on this together with designer Marjolein Vermeulen (on behalf of M.V.). I also worked with Tabo Goudswaard and Vera Winthagen on the A9 project case study in chapter 4, for which Frans de Kock, Lammert Postma and Marcel Hoogsteder were important partners on the client side.

In the project on climate adaptation (see section 6.1), Peter Glas played an important role as the director of de Dommel water board, while the official clients Karla Niggebrugge and Dick Boland were absolute stars in building a large coalition that allowed us to set up a great project. There were numerous designers involved in this, three of whom — Maartje van Gestel, Dick Rijken and Hugo Schuitemaker — I'd like to thank in particular.

The Landbouw Innovatie Campus from section 6.4 was a long-term project in which public administrator Anne-Marie Spierings and official client Pieter de Boer played decisive roles. A large number of designers were involved at Landbouw Innovatie Campus. Without them, I wouldn't have been able to set up this project. The creators of the 'doehetzelfkip' are Sascha Landshoff and Vera Bachrach, who were supported from the official client side by Wim Coenraadts.

And finally, Maybourhood, which has become an ongoing research project that has been applied in many places both in the Netherlands and abroad. I developed the basis of this project with Tabo Goudswaard. Pim Marcus was the official client for the first four experiments. Without his trust, it would never have taken off as it has.

Many colleagues at Twynstra Gudde participated in our projects, helped develop our concepts and introduced us at clients.

Students of the Design Academy Eindhoven have also made a worthwhile contribution to various projects.

I've also greatly enjoyed working with Paul Gofferjé, Martijn Engelbregt, Henk Keizer, Yuri Veerman, Manon van Hoeckel, Jan Dirk van der Burg, the people at VanBerlo, Pim Meijer and Anne-Marth Kuilder over the past few years.

Thanks also to all the interviewees; although not all of you made it into this book, that doesn't have anything to do with you. There's only so much that one book can share.

I'd also like to thank everyone I asked to give me feedback on particular sections: Anne Marijn Koppen, Roos Knap, Mieke Moor, Judith Spijkerman, Annick de Vries, Niels Vrije, Hanna

Boersema-Vermeer, Martine de Jong, Marcel de Rooij, Joost Voerman, Dick Rijken, Hans Vermaak and Rudy Kor.

Many thanks to Marlieke Kieboom, who cast her critical eye over the entire book and helped to fine-tune it.

Many thanks also to Kees Dorst, who talked me into the process of writing this book at a bar in Sydney, often shared his thoughts, wrote the foreword and even drew a hippo for me. And when I was being too ambitious, he'd say "save that for your second book."

The book was edited by Henk Bouwmeester and translated by Johann Migchels on behalf of Powerling. It was designed by Floris van Driel. The font used in this book was developed by Mateo Broillet.

The book was published by Bionda Dias of BIS and promoted by Sara van de Ven of BIS and Esther van Koot of Twynstra Gudde. Thank you all.

And finally, my heartfelt thanks to friends and family and especially Marieke Helmus, Jiri & Josha ♥

COLOPHON

GRAPHIC DESIGN
Floris van Driel

FONTS USED
Nero Regular by Mateo Broillet
AG Buch Regular by Berthold
GT America Mono Regular by Grilli Type

NOVEMBER 2018

CONTACT
André Schaminée
www.twynstragudde.nl/designing
www.andreschaminee.nl

BIS Publishers
Building Het Sieraad
Postjesweg 1
1057 DT Amsterdam
The Netherlands
T +31 (0)20 515 02 30
bis@bispublishers.com
www.bispublishers.com

ISBN 978 90 6369 497 5

Copyright © 2018 André Schaminée
and BIS Publishers.